TEST KITCHEN
FAVORITES

TASTE OF HOME BOOKS • RDA ENTHUSIAST BRANDS, LLC • MILWAUKEE, WI

Taste *of* Home

ISBN:
978-1-61765-874-7
Component Number:
116700089H
LOCC: 2019934825

Deputy Editor: Mark Hagen
Senior Art Director: Raeann Thompson
Senior Designer: Courtney Lovetere
Designer: Jazmin Delgado
Senior Copy Editor: Dulcie Shoener
Editorial Intern: Salam Fatayer

Cover Photography
Photographer: Grace Natoli Sheldon
Senior Set Stylist: Melissa Franco
Food Stylist: Kathryn Conrad

Pictured on front cover:
Overnight Cinnamon Rolls, p. 24

Pictured on title page:
Mile-High Chicken Potpie, p. 17

Pictured on back cover:
Pumpkin Pecan Whoopie Pies, p. 10
Spaghetti & Meatball Soup, p. 9
Reuben Salad in a Jar, p. 45

Printed in USA
1 3 5 7 9 10 8 6 4 2

Simply the Best

Family time is truly special in my house, so I always try to set the table with the best foods possible—the tastiest, the prettiest and the most memorable. As culinary director of the *Taste of Home* Test Kitchen, I get a sneak peek at (and taste of) all the wonderful recipes our readers share with us.

Over the past 25 years, our Test Kitchen has tested, tasted and approved more than 75,000 recipes. From all-time standbys to trendy new bites, we've seen and tasted them all! (Tough job, huh?) That's why I'm so excited about this incredible all-new collection.

We asked our Test Kitchen pros which dishes made their list of all-time favorites—which recipes they actually took home and served their own families. Next, we put those tasty specialties into this handy resource. Now you can find those best-of-the-best entrees, appetizers, desserts and more in one spot.

With *Taste of Home Test Kitchen Favorites*, you'll enjoy 142 of the recipes our staff deemed the best. You'll discover mouthwatering sensations developed by our own experts as well as must-try dishes sent by readers. For example, turn to page 10 and you'll find Pumpkin Pecan Whoopie Pies shared by Rashanda Cobbins, a food editor on our team. I'm obsessed with the Raspberry Peach Puff Pancake on page 21. That eye-opening dish was the result of a team effort in our Test Kitchen. On page 59, you'll enjoy Roasted Chicken with Rosemary. It was submitted by Isabel Zienkosky, a home cook from Salt Lake City. It instantly became a hit with all of us!

This book begins with a bonus section of recipes that come directly from the *Taste of Home* staff. Let me introduce you to some of the folks I work with and share their all-time best dishes. Not only do they serve these foods in their own homes, but their recipes have proven quite popular with our readers.

DISHING WITH

Sarah Farmer
Taste of Home Culinary Director

You'll also find chapters featuring our breakfast favorites, five-star appetizers, savory entrees and, of course, the heavenly sweets we adore.

Your family deserves the best, so why not serve tried-and-true winners every night of the week? With *Taste of Home Test Kitchen Favorites* at your fingertips, I'm sure that our most-loved dishes are going to become new standbys in your home as well.

Happy cooking,

Sarah Farmer

Take a Peek Inside Our Test Kitchen

Family cooks sharing their all-time best recipes—that's long been the hallmark of *Taste of Home*. And while we couldn't do what we do without these gracious home cooks, it's our Test Kitchen team that makes sure each recipe we receive will turn out perfect in homes from coast to coast.

Each year the *Taste of Home* Test Kitchen staff receives about 6,000 recipes, and tests about half of those.

Every submission is reviewed by food editors and culinary assistants. They check that each recipe is complete, calls for common ingredients, offers easy-to-follow directions and fits with the *Taste of Home* family of recipes. In addition, they look to be sure *Taste of Home* has not published a similar recipe in the past.

Once it's approved, a recipe is scheduled for testing and the cooking begins! It should come as no surprise that every weekday our Test Kitchen is busy baking, frying, simmering, mixing and preparing all sorts of wonderful dishes. Just consider these facts:

• The Test Kitchen uses 382 pounds of butter per year.

• The cooks go through 600 pounds of flour every month.

• Roughly 98 pounds of bacon sizzle to perfection in the Test Kitchen annually.

• Our prep cooks slice and dice about 441 onions and 294 lemons each year.

On average, the Test Kitchen hosts two taste-testing sessions per day for a panel of test cooks and editors. After tasting an item, they discuss it in detail—flavor, texture, cooking method, visual appeal and more.

Every recipe needs a thumbs-up approval from the panel before it's marked "ready for publication" in the extensive *Taste of Home* recipe database. There are more than 229,000 recipes in our database. In fact, if we wrote each recipe on a 3x5-inch index card laid end to end, the cards would cover 318 football fields!

As soon as a recipe is scheduled for its initial publication, it's slated to appear on a set in the *Taste of Home* Photo Studio. A special prep kitchen, located within the studio, ensures our team of food stylists will have each dish ready for its time in the spotlight. Our photographers keep busy, shooting foods an average of eight hours per day.

In addition to appearing in *Taste of Home* magazine, recipes are posted on *TasteofHome.com* as well as social media sites, where they can receive up to 20 million page views.

Similarly, recipes are published in our cookbooks as well as special-interest publications found at grocery stores and wherever cooking magazines are sold.

Why do so many people send their recipes to the *Taste of Home* Test Kitchen each year? Many are entries for contests and others are submitted for particular magazine features. Most, however, come from home cooks who simply want to share their love of food with families just like yours!

Contents

Want More Behind the Scenes?

LIKE US: facebook.com/tasteofhome | **PIN US:** pinterest.com/taste_of_home
FOLLOW US: @tasteofhome | **TWEET US:** twitter.com/tasteofhome

TO FIND A RECIPE:
tasteofhome.com

TO SUBMIT A RECIPE:
tasteofhome.com/submit

TO FIND OUT ABOUT OTHER *TASTE OF HOME* PRODUCTS:
shoptasteofhome.com

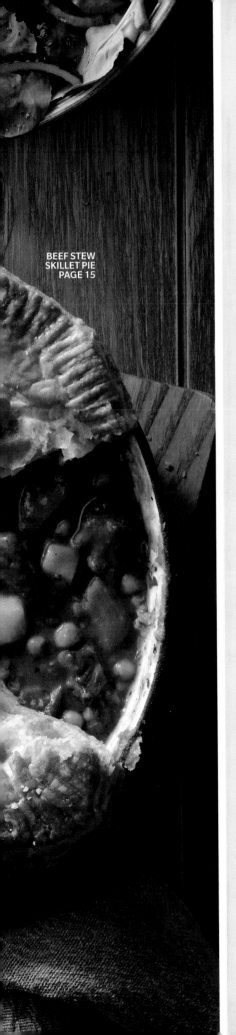

BEEF STEW
SKILLET PIE
PAGE 15

BONUS: THE TEST KITCHEN'S
All-Time Favorites

Grab your stretchy pants, because this chapter features mouthwatering recipes actually dreamed up by the *Taste of Home* staff. Turn the page and you'll find appetizers, entrees and sweets our team created, the Test Kitchen approved and everyone loved. Discover a new family favorite tonight!

DISHING WITH

Susan Stetzel
Associate Food Editor

A couple of nights a week our family ends up eating in shifts because everyone is going every which way at the same time. Having my hearty soup simmering in the slow cooker is an easy way to give them all a warm meal.

**SPAGHETTI &
MEATBALL SOUP**

SPAGHETTI & MEATBALL SOUP

—Susan Stetzel, Gainesville, NY

PREP: 45 min. • **COOK:** 6¼ hours
MAKES: 8 servings (3¼ qt.)

- 1 cup soft bread crumbs
- ¾ cup 2% milk
- 2 large eggs, lightly beaten
- ½ cup freshly grated Parmesan cheese
- ¾ tsp. salt
- ½ tsp. garlic powder
- ½ tsp. pepper
- 2 lbs. ground Italian sausage

SOUP

- 4 cups beef stock
- 1 jar (24 oz.) marinara sauce
- 3 cups water
- 1 tsp. dried basil
   Parmesan rind, optional
- 8 oz. angel hair pasta, broken
   into 1½-in. pieces
   Additional freshly grated Parmesan
   cheese, optional

1. Preheat oven to 400°. In a large bowl, mix bread crumbs and milk. Let stand 5 minutes; drain. Stir in eggs, cheese and seasonings. Add sausage; mix lightly but thoroughly. Shape into 1-in. balls. Place meatballs on a greased rack in a 15x10x1-in. baking pan. Bake 12-15 minutes or until cooked through.
2. Transfer meatballs to a 6-qt. slow cooker. Add stock, marinara sauce, water, basil and, if desired, Parmesan rind. Cook, covered, on low 6-8 hours.
3. Discard Parmesan rind. Stir in pasta; cook, covered, on high 15-20 minutes longer or until pasta is tender. If desired, serve with additional cheese.
NOTE: To make soft bread crumbs, tear bread into pieces and place in a food processor or blender. Cover and pulse until crumbs form. One slice of bread yields ½ to ¾ cup crumbs.
1½ CUPS: 394 cal., 26g fat (9g sat. fat), 95mg chol., 1452mg sod., 23g carb. (9g sugars, 2g fiber), 17g pro.

HOMEMADE LEMON CURD

HOMEMADE LEMON CURD

—Mark Hagen, Milwaukee, WI

PREP: 20 min. + chilling • **MAKES:** 1⅔ cups

- 3 large eggs
- 1 cup sugar
- ½ cup lemon juice (about 2 lemons)
- ¼ cup butter, cubed
- 1 Tbsp. grated lemon zest

In a small heavy saucepan over medium heat, whisk eggs, sugar and lemon juice until blended. Add butter and lemon zest; cook, whisking constantly, until the mixture is thickened and coats the back of a metal spoon. Transfer to a small bowl; cool for 10 minutes. Refrigerate, covered, until cold.
2 TBSP.: 110 cal., 5g fat (3g sat. fat), 52mg chol., 45mg sod., 16g carb. (16g sugars, 0 fiber), 2g pro.
LIME CURD: Substitute lime juice and zest for lemon juice and zest. Proceed as directed.

DISHING WITH

Mark Hagen

Deputy Editor

Lemon curd is a scrumptious spread for scones, biscuits or other baked goods. You can find it in larger grocery stores alongside the jams and jellies or with the baking supplies, but I like making it from scratch. It's so easy!

DISHING WITH

Rachel Bernhard Seis
Senior Editor

These spiked gelatin squares get any party started! For a more traditional shot-style look, pour the mixture into 2-ounce plastic cups and refrigerate until set.

SPICED APPLE CIDER JELLY SHOTS
—Rachel Bernard Seis, Milwaukee, WI

PREP: 10 min. • **COOK:** 5 min. + chilling
MAKES: 64 squares

- 1½ cups cold apple cider or juice
- 4 envelopes unflavored gelatin
- 1 cup sugar
- 1½ cups ginger-flavored vodka
- 2 tsp. Angostura bitters
- 2 Tbsp. cinnamon sugar
  Thinly sliced apple, optional

1. Pour apple cider into a large saucepan and sprinkle gelatin over top; let stand, without stirring, until gelatin softens, about 5 minutes. Whisk in sugar. Heat and stir over low heat until sugar and gelatin are completely dissolved, 8-10 minutes (do not boil); remove from heat. Stir in vodka; pour mixture into a 9-in. square baking pan coated with cooking spray. Refrigerate, uncovered, until mixture is firm, about 2 hours.
2. To unmold, run a sharp knife along edges of gelatin; invert onto a cutting board and lift off pan. Cut into 64 squares; brush tops with bitters and sprinkle with cinnamon sugar. If desired, garnish with apple slices.
1 SQUARE: 28 cal., 0 fat (0 sat. fat), 0 chol., 1mg sod., 4g carb. (4g sugars, 0 fiber), 0 pro.

SPICED APPLE CIDER JELLY SHOTS

PUMPKIN PECAN WHOOPIE PIES
—Rashanda Cobbins, Milwaukee, WI

PREP: 30 min. • **BAKE:** 10 min./batch + cooling
MAKES: 20 whoopie pies

- 3¼ cups all-purpose flour
- 1½ cups sugar
- 2 tsp. baking powder
- 2 tsp. baking soda
- 1½ tsp. ground cinnamon
- 1 tsp. ground nutmeg
- 1 tsp. ground cloves
- ½ tsp. salt
- 5 large eggs
- 1 can (15 oz.) solid-pack pumpkin
- ½ cup water
- ½ cup canola oil
- 1 tsp. vanilla extract
FILLING
- 6 Tbsp. all-purpose flour
- 1 dash salt
- 1 cup plus 2 Tbsp. unsweetened almond milk

DISHING WITH

Rashanda Cobbins
Food Editor

Let's review: Pumpkin...pecan... whoopie pies. What's not to love? I hope you like them as much as I do.

- 1½ cups shortening
- 3 cups confectioners' sugar
- 3 tsp. vanilla extract
  Toasted chopped pecans, miniature semisweet chocolate chips and ground cinnamon, optional

1. In a large bowl, combine the flour, sugar, baking powder, baking soda, cinnamon, nutmeg, cloves and salt. In another bowl, whisk the eggs, pumpkin, water, oil and vanilla. Gently stir into dry ingredients just until moistened.
2. Drop by 2 tablespoonfuls 2 in. apart onto parchment-lined baking sheets. Bake at 350° for 8-10 minutes. Carefully remove to wire racks to cool.
3. For filling, combine flour and salt in a small saucepan. Gradually whisk in the milk until smooth; bring to a boil over medium-high heat. Reduce heat to medium; cook and stir until thickened, about 2 minutes. Refrigerate, covered, until completely cooled.
4. In another bowl, beat the shortening, confectioners' sugar and vanilla until smooth. Add chilled milk mixture; beat until light and fluffy, about 7 minutes. Spread about 3 Tbsp. filling on the bottoms of half of the cookies; cover with remaining cookies. Store in the refrigerator. If desired, roll the filled pies in pecans or chocolate chips and sprinkle with additional cinnamon.
1 WHOOPIE PIE: 424 cal., 22g fat (5g sat. fat), 47mg chol., 277mg sod., 53g carb. (34g sugars, 1g fiber), 4g pro.

PUMPKIN PECAN WHOOPIE PIES

FAJITA IN A BOWL

Peggy Woodward
Senior Food Editor

I head out to the grill to char broil miniature peppers, onions and corn for an awesome steak salad that's both fresh and hearty.

FAJITA IN A BOWL

—Peggy Woodward, Shullsburg, WI

TAKES: 30 min. • **MAKES:** 4 servings

- 1 Tbsp. brown sugar
- 1 Tbsp. chili powder
- ½ tsp. salt
- 1 beef flank steak (1 lb.)
- 12 miniature sweet peppers, halved and seeded
- 1 medium red onion, cut into thin wedges
- 2 cups cherry tomatoes
- 2 medium ears sweet corn, husks removed

SALAD
- 12 cups torn mixed salad greens
- 1 cup fresh cilantro leaves
- ½ cup reduced-fat lime vinaigrette
  Optional ingredients: cotija cheese, lime wedges and tortillas

1. In a small bowl, mix brown sugar, chili powder and salt. Rub onto both sides of the flank steak.

2. Place peppers and onion on a grilling grid; place on grill rack over medium heat. Grill, covered, 9-11 minutes or until crisp-tender, stirring occasionally; add tomatoes during the last 2 minutes. Remove from grill.

3. Place steak and corn directly on grill rack; close lid. Grill steak 8-10 minutes on each side or until a thermometer reads 135° for medium-rare; grill corn 10-12 minutes or until lightly charred, turning occasionally.

4. Divide greens and cilantro among four bowls. Cut corn from cobs and thinly slice steak across the grain; place in bowls. Top with vegetables; drizzle with vinaigrette. If desired, serve with cheese, lime and tortillas.

NOTE: If you do not have a grilling grid, use a disposable foil pan with holes poked into the bottom with a meat fork.

1 SALAD: 351 cal., 14g fat (5g sat. fat), 54mg chol., 862mg sod., 33g carb. (16g sugars, 7g fiber), 28g pro.

SKILLET CHOCOLATE CHUNK WALNUT BLONDIES

Put these beauties out at a potluck and you'll find only crumbs left over when it's time to head home. Everyone will ask who made those delectable blondies, so be sure to bring copies of the recipe!
—Peggy Woodward, Shullsburg, WI

PREP: 15 min.
BAKE: 30 min.
MAKES: 2 dozen

- 1 cup butter, melted
- 2 cups packed brown sugar
- 2 tsp. vanilla extract
- 2 large eggs
- 2 cups all-purpose flour
- ½ cup ground walnuts
- 1 tsp. baking powder
- ½ tsp. salt
- ⅛ tsp. baking soda
- 1 cup chopped walnuts, toasted
- 1 cup semisweet chocolate chunks

1. Preheat oven to 350°. Grease three 6½-in. cast-iron skillets.

2. In a large bowl, mix butter, brown sugar and vanilla until blended. Add eggs, one at a time, whisking to blend after each addition. In another bowl, mix flour, ground walnuts, baking powder, salt and baking soda; stir into butter mixture. Fold in walnuts and chocolate chunks.

3. Spread into skillets. Bake until a toothpick inserted in center comes out with moist crumbs and top is golden, 30-35 minutes. Cool slightly; serve warm.

1 PIECE: 262 cal., 15g fat (7g sat. fat), 36mg chol., 149mg sod., 32g carb. (22g sugars, 1g fiber), 3g pro.

SKILLET CHOCOLATE CHUNK WALNUT BLONDIES

**APPLE CINNAMON
OVERNIGHT OATS**

3 cups beef stock
1 bottle (12 oz.) beer
2 cans (14½ oz. each) fire-roasted
    diced tomatoes, undrained
1 can (16 oz.) kidney beans, drained
3 Tbsp. masa harina
    American cheese slices, sour cream,
    shredded cheddar cheese, diced red
    onion, Fritos corn chips, optional

1. Combine chiles and enough boiling water to cover; let stand until softened, about 15 minutes. Drain, reserving ⅓ cup of the soaking liquid. Discard stems and seeds. Process chiles, tomato paste, garlic and reserved liquid until smooth.
2. In a small skillet, toast chili powder, paprika and cumin over medium heat until aromatic, 3-4 minutes; remove and set aside. In a Dutch oven, cook and stir ground beef and steak seasoning over medium-high heat until the beef is no longer pink, about 5 minutes; remove and drain.
3. Sprinkle steak cubes with 1 tsp. each salt and pepper. In same Dutch oven, brown beef in batches in 1 Tbsp. oil over medium-high heat; remove and set aside. Saute onion and poblano pepper in the remaining 1 Tbsp. oil until tender, about 5 minutes. Stir in toasted spices, oregano and pepper flakes. Add the cooked meats along with stock, beer, tomatoes, beans, remaining salt and pepper, and chile paste mixture. Cook over medium heat 20 minutes; reduce heat to low. Stir in masa and simmer 30-45 minutes longer. Serve with desired toppings.
FREEZE OPTION: Freeze cooled chili in freezer containers. To use, partially thaw in refrigerator overnight. Heat through in a saucepan, stirring occasionally; add a little broth or water if necessary.
1¾ CUPS: 473 cal., 20g fat (6g sat. fat), 103mg chol., 1554mg sod., 29g carb. (8g sugars, 7g fiber), 41g pro.

TEST KITCHEN TIP
Masa harina is a ground corn flour often used in Mexican cooking. Adding it at the end of this recipe helps thicken the chili, giving it the perfect body and a wonderfully subtle corn flavor.

APPLE CINNAMON OVERNIGHT OATS

Many folks love this oatmeal cold, but I like to heat it up a little since I'm not a big fan of it right out of the fridge. Add a handful of nuts for a little crunch, additional flavor and extra health benefits.
—Sarah Farmer, Waukesha, WI

- -

PREP: 5 min. + chilling • **MAKES:** 1 serving

½ cup old-fashioned oats
½ medium Gala or Honeycrisp
    apple, chopped
1 Tbsp. raisins
1 cup 2% milk
¼ tsp. ground cinnamon
    Dash salt
    Toasted, chopped nuts, optional

In a small container or mason jar, combine all ingredients. Seal; refrigerate overnight.
1½ CUPS: 349 cal., 8g fat (4g sat. fat), 20mg chol., 263mg sod., 59g carb. (28g sugars, 7g fiber), 14g pro.

FAVORITE CHILI
—Sarah Farmer, Waukesha, WI

- -

PREP: 20 min. • **COOK:** 1 hour 20 min.
MAKES: 8 servings

3 dried ancho or guajillo chiles
1 to 2 cups boiling water
2 Tbsp. tomato paste
3 garlic cloves
¼ cup chili powder
1½ tsp. smoked paprika
2 tsp. ground cumin
1 lb. ground beef
1½ tsp. Montreal steak seasoning
2 lbs. beef tri-tip roast, cut
    into ½-in. cubes
2 tsp. salt, divided
2 tsp. coarsely ground pepper, divided
2 Tbsp. canola oil, divided
1 large onion, chopped (about 2 cups)
1 poblano pepper, seeded
    and chopped
1 tsp. dried oregano
1½ tsp. crushed red pepper flakes

FAVORITE CHILI

DISHING WITH

Sarah Farmer
Culinary Director

My dad and my father-in-law are
the gurus in our chili-loving clan.
Inspired by the fresh and fragrant
chile peppers at the Santa Fe
farmers market I visited during
my honeymoon in New Mexico,
I felt it was time to introduce
them to my spicy, meaty version
with a touch of masa harina.

MARSHMALLOW SKEWER POPS

MARSHMALLOW SKEWER POPS
—James Schend, Pleasant Prairie, WI

TAKES: 10 min. • **MAKES:** 12 pops

- 2 **cups semisweet chocolate chips**
- 2 **Tbsp. shortening**
- 36 **large marshmallows**
- 12 **lollipop sticks**
  Assorted colored candy coating, melted

In a microwave, melt the chocolate and the shortening; stir until smooth. Skewer three marshmallows on each stick. Spoon the chocolate over marshmallows; set on waxed paper until firm. Drizzle with melted colored candy coating.

1 POP: 74 cal., 3g fat (2g sat. fat), 0 chol., 7mg sod., 12g carb. (9g sugars, 1g fiber), 1g pro.

DISHING WITH

James Schend
Deputy Editor

These marshmallow pops are a hit with the kids. Let them drizzle away with their favorite colors!

DISHING WITH

Stephanie Marchese
Visual Production Director

My brother, Joe, and I created this lasagna based on our mom's recipe. It's a family favorite at Christmas, thanks to all of the special ingredients that make it *magnifico*.

THE BEST EVER LASAGNA
—Stephanie Marchese, Whitefish Bay, WI

PREP: 2¾ hours • **BAKE:** 1 hour + standing
MAKES: 15 servings

- 1 **medium onion, chopped**
- 2 **Tbsp. olive oil**
- 4 **garlic cloves, minced**
- 1 **can (6 oz.) tomato paste**
- 2 **cans (28 oz. each) crushed tomatoes in puree**
- 6 **cups water**
- 1 **cup chopped fresh basil**
- 2¼ **tsp. sugar, divided**
- 1 **tsp. salt**
- 1 **lb. bulk Italian sausage**
- 4 **Italian sausage links**
- 1 **carton (16 oz.) whole milk ricotta cheese**
- 8 **cups shredded mozzarella cheese, divided**
- 1 **large egg, beaten**
- ¼ **tsp. dried basil**
- 12 **sheets no-cook lasagna noodles**
- 21 **slices provolone cheese**
- ⅓ **cup grated Parmesan cheese**

1. In a Dutch oven, cook onion in olive oil over medium heat until tender, 4-5 minutes. Add garlic; cook 1 minute. Stir in tomato paste and cook, stirring constantly, until fragrant, 3-4 minutes. Add the crushed tomatoes, water, fresh basil, 2 tsp. sugar and salt. Bring to a boil; reduce heat. Simmer 1 hour, stirring occasionally.

2. Meanwhile, cook the sausage in a skillet over medium heat until no longer pink, breaking into crumbles, 8-10 minutes; drain. Add to sauce; simmer until mixture is thickened, about 1 hour longer.

3. While sauce simmers, preheat oven to 350°. Place sausage links on a rimmed baking sheet; roast until cooked through, 35-40 minutes. Remove and let cool slightly; slice into ¼-in.-thick pieces.

4. In a small bowl, mix ricotta cheese, 1 cup mozzarella cheese, egg, dried basil and remaining sugar.

5. In a greased 13x9-in. baking dish, spread 2 cups sauce. Arrange four noodles over sauce; spread with a third of the ricotta mixture. Add seven provolone slices, a third of the sausage links and 1½ cups mozzarella cheese. Repeat layers two more times, using only 1 cup sauce per layer. Spread with 2 cups sauce (reserve remaining sauce for serving on the side), remaining 2½ cups mozzarella cheese and the Parmesan cheese (dish will be full).

6. Place dish on a rimmed baking sheet and bake, uncovered, until bubbly and deep golden brown, 60-65 minutes. Let stand for 15 minutes before serving. Serve with the remaining meat sauce.

1 PIECE: 509 cal., 33g fat (15g sat. fat), 106mg chol., 1185mg sod., 27g carb. (9g sugars, 3g fiber), 29g pro.

THE BEST EVER LASAGNA

BLACKBERRY GRILLED
CHEESE SANDWICH

DISHING WITH

Josh Rink
Food Stylist

If you're looking for a gourmet
grilled cheese recipe, your search
is over! With five kinds of cheese
and fresh blackberries, my
sandwich is impressive enough
to even serve to guests.

BLACKBERRY GRILLED CHEESE SANDWICH

—Josh Rink, Milwaukee, WI

PREP: 30 min. • **COOK:** 10 min.
MAKES: 4 servings

- 6   Tbsp. butter, softened, divided
- 8   slices sourdough bread
- ½   cup shredded sharp white cheddar cheese
- ½   cup shredded Monterey Jack cheese
- ½   cup shredded Gruyere cheese
- 3   Tbsp. finely shredded Manchego or Parmesan cheese
- 3   Tbsp. mayonnaise
- ⅛   tsp. onion powder
- 4   oz. Brie cheese, sliced, rind removed
- 1   cup fresh blackberries

1. Spread half the butter over one side of bread slices. In a large skillet, toast bread, buttered side down, over medium-low heat until golden brown, 2-3 minutes.
2. In a small bowl, combine cheddar, Monterey Jack and Gruyere cheeses. In another bowl, mix together Manchego cheese, mayonnaise, remaining 3 Tbsp. butter and the onion powder.
3. On four slices of toast, layer Brie cheese, cheddar cheese mixture and blackberries. Top with remaining slices, toasted side down. Spread outsides of sandwiches with mayonnaise mixture. Toast sandwiches over medium heat until golden brown and cheese is melted, 5-6 minutes on each side. Serve immediately.

1 SANDWICH: 674 cal., 50g fat (27g sat. fat), 122mg chol., 1018mg sod., 34g carb. (5g sugars, 3g fiber), 25g pro.

BEEF STEW SKILLET PIE

I rely on puff pastry for an eye-catching topping for this hearty skillet potpie.
—Josh Rink, Milwaukee, WI

PREP: 1½ hours • **BAKE:** 30 min. + standing
MAKES: 6 servings

- 6   Tbsp. all-purpose flour, divided
- 1½ tsp. salt
- ½   tsp. pepper
- 1   lb. boneless beef round steak, cut into 1-in. pieces
- 2   Tbsp. canola oil
- 1   large onion, chopped
- 2   garlic cloves, minced
- ¼   cup dry red wine
- 2   cups beef broth, divided
- 1   Tbsp. tomato paste
- ½   tsp. Italian seasoning
- ½   tsp. dried basil
- 1   bay leaf
- 2   medium potatoes, cubed
- 3   large carrots, peeled and sliced
- ½   cup frozen peas
- 2   Tbsp. minced fresh parsley
- 1   sheet frozen puff pastry, thawed
- 1   large egg, beaten

1. In a large resealable container, combine 3 Tbsp. flour, salt and pepper. Add beef in batches; shake to coat. Invert a 10-in. ovenproof skillet onto parchment; trace circle around pan ¼ in. larger than rim. Cut out circle and set aside. In same skillet, saute beef in oil until browned. Add onion and garlic; cook and stir until onion is tender. Add wine, stirring to loosen browned bits.
2. Combine 1½ cups broth, tomato paste, Italian seasoning and basil; stir into skillet. Add bay leaf. Bring to a boil. Reduce heat;

cover and simmer until meat is tender, about 45 minutes. Add the potatoes and carrots; cook until vegetables are tender, about 20-25 minutes longer.
3. Meanwhile, roll out puff pastry to fit skillet using parchment circle as a guide; carefully cut venting slits in pastry. Keep chilled until ready to use.
4. Combine the remaining flour and broth until smooth; gradually stir into skillet. Bring to a boil; cook and stir for 2 minutes or until thickened and bubbly. Discard bay leaf. Stir in peas and parsley.
5. Brush some of the beaten egg around edge of skillet to help pastry adhere; carefully place pastry over filling. Using a fork, press pastry firmly onto rim of pan; brush with egg. Bake pie at 425° until pastry is dark golden brown, 30-35 minutes. Let stand for 10 minutes before serving.

1 SLICE: 473 cal., 19g fat (4g sat. fat), 73mg chol., 1088mg sod., 49g carb. (4g sugars, 6g fiber), 25g pro.

BEEF STEW
SKILLET PIE

DISHING WITH

Shannon Roum
Senior Food Stylist

Here, bone-in chicken brings a flavor that's enhanced by herbs, lemon and hearty vegetables.

GARLICKY
CHICKEN
DINNER

GARLICKY CHICKEN DINNER

—Shannon Roum, Cudahy, WI

PREP: 25 min. • **BAKE:** 45 min.
MAKES: 8 servings

- 1¼ lbs. small red potatoes, quartered
- 4 medium carrots, cut into ½-in. slices
- 1 medium red onion, cut into thin wedges
- 1 Tbsp. olive oil
- 6 garlic cloves, minced
- 2 tsp. minced fresh thyme, divided
- 1½ tsp. salt, divided
- 1 tsp. pepper, divided
- 1 tsp. paprika
- 4 chicken drumsticks
- 4 bone-in chicken thighs
- 1 small lemon, sliced
- 1 pkg. (5 oz.) fresh spinach

1. Preheat oven to 425°. In a large bowl, combine potatoes, carrots, onion, oil, garlic, 1 tsp. thyme, ¾ tsp. salt and ½ tsp. pepper; toss to coat.
2. Transfer mixture to a 15x10x1-in. baking pan coated with cooking spray.
3. In a small bowl, mix paprika and the remaining thyme, salt and pepper. Sprinkle chicken with paprika mixture; arrange over vegetables. Top with lemon slices. Roast until a thermometer inserted in chicken reads 170°-175° and vegetables are just tender, 35-40 minutes.
4. Remove chicken to a serving platter; keep warm. Top vegetables with spinach. Roast until vegetables are tender and spinach is wilted, 8-10 minutes longer. Stir vegetables to combine; serve with chicken.

1 PIECE CHICKEN WITH 1 CUP VEGETABLES: 264 cal., 12g fat (3g sat. fat), 64mg chol., 548mg sod., 18g carb. (3g sugars, 3g fiber), 21g pro. **DIABETIC EXCHANGES:** 3 medium-fat meat, 1 starch, 1 vegetable, ½ fat.

MILE-HIGH CHICKEN POTPIE

MILE-HIGH CHICKEN POTPIE

Classic chicken potpie gets extra homey when it's loaded with a creamy filling and baked tall in a springform pan. I find this deep-dish marvel perfect for cozy Sunday dinners with the family.
—Shannon Roum, Cudahy, WI

PREP: 40 min. + chilling
BAKE: 50 min. + standing
MAKES: 6 servings

- 1 large egg, separated
- 4 to 6 Tbsp. cold water, divided
- 2 cups all-purpose flour
- ¼ tsp. salt
- ⅔ cup cold butter, cubed

FILLING
- 3 Tbsp. butter
- 2 medium potatoes, peeled and cut into ½-in. cubes
- 4 medium carrots, thinly sliced
- 2 celery ribs, finely chopped
- ¼ cup finely chopped onion
- 3 Tbsp. all-purpose flour
- 2 Tbsp. chicken bouillon granules
- 1½ tsp. dried tarragon
- ½ tsp. coarsely ground pepper
- 1½ cups half-and-half cream
- 2½ cups cubed cooked chicken
- 1½ cups fresh peas or frozen peas
- ½ to 1 tsp. celery seed

1. In a small bowl, beat egg yolk with 2 Tbsp. water. In a large bowl, combine flour and salt; cut in butter until crumbly. Gradually add yolk mixture, tossing with a fork; add additional water 1 Tbsp. at a time, as needed, until dough forms a ball. Divide dough into two portions, one with three-quarters of the dough and one with the remainder. Shape each into a disk; cover and refrigerate 1 hour or overnight.
2. For filling, in a Dutch oven, melt butter. Saute potatoes, carrots, celery and onion until crisp-tender, 5-7 minutes. Stir in flour, bouillon, tarragon and pepper. Gradually stir in cream. Bring to a boil; cook and stir until thickened, about 2 minutes. Stir in chicken and peas; set aside to cool completely. On a lightly floured surface, roll out larger portion of dough to fit bottom and up the sides of an 8-in. springform pan; place dough in pan. Add cooled filling. Roll remaining dough to fit over the top; place over filling. Trim, seal and flute edge; cut slits in top. Chill at least 1 hour.
3. Lightly beat egg white with 1 tsp. water. Brush over the top crust; sprinkle with celery seed. Place pie on a rimmed baking tray.
4. Bake at 400° until crust is golden brown and filling is bubbly, 50-55 minutes. Cool potpie on a wire rack for at least 30 minutes before serving.

1 PIECE: 700 cal., 38g fat (22g sat. fat), 183mg chol., 1282mg sod., 58g carb. (8g sugars, 6g fiber), 29g pro.

OVERNIGHT CINNAMON
ROLLS, PAGE 24

FAVORITE

Breakfasts

When it comes to daybreak eats, our Test Kitchen
staff has a long list of standbys. Check out their
best-loved eye-openers—perfect for hurried
weekdays as well as quaint Sunday brunches.

APPLE-SAGE
SAUSAGE PATTIES

APPLE-SAGE SAUSAGE PATTIES

Apple and sausage naturally go together. Add sage, and you truly have a standout breakfast patty. They're freezer-friendly, so I make them ahead and grab when needed.
—Scarlett Elrod, Newnan, GA

PREP: 35 min. + chilling
COOK: 10 min./batch • **MAKES:** 16 patties

- 1 large apple
- 1 large egg, lightly beaten
- ½ cup chopped fresh parsley
- 3 to 4 Tbsp. minced fresh sage
- 2 garlic cloves, minced
- 1¼ tsp. salt
- ½ tsp. pepper
- ½ tsp. crushed red pepper flakes
- 1¼ lbs. lean ground turkey
- 6 tsp. olive oil, divided

1. Peel and coarsely shred apple; place apple in a colander over a plate. Let stand about 15 minutes. Gently squeeze and blot dry with paper towels.
2. In a large bowl, combine egg, parsley, sage, garlic, seasonings and apple. Add turkey; mix lightly but thoroughly. Shape into sixteen 2-in. patties. Place patties on waxed paper-lined baking sheets. Refrigerate, covered, 8 hours or overnight.
3. In a large nonstick skillet, heat 2 tsp. oil over medium heat. In batches, cook patties 3-4 minutes on each side or until golden brown and a thermometer reads 165°, adding additional oil as needed.
FREEZE OPTION: Place uncooked patties on waxed paper-lined baking sheets; wrap and freeze until firm. Remove from pans and transfer to a freezer container; return to freezer. To use, cook frozen patties as directed, increasing time to 4-5 minutes on each side.
1 PATTY: 79 cal., 5g fat (1g sat. fat), 36mg chol., 211mg sod., 2g carb. (1g sugars, 0 fiber), 8g pro. **DIABETIC EXCHANGES:** 1 lean meat, ½ fat.

TEST KITCHEN TIP
Customize the breakfast patties to your liking. Don't care for red pepper flakes? Leave them out. Try adding a dash of thyme or mix in a bit of onion powder. Replace some of the apple with pear.

RASBERRY PEACH PUFF PANCAKE

RASPBERRY PEACH PUFF PANCAKE

Here's a simple, satisfying treat that's perfect for when you have company for brunch. It's elegant enough that you can even serve it for dessert at other meals.
—*Taste of Home* Test Kitchen

PREP: 15 min. • **BAKE:** 20 min.
MAKES: 4 servings

- 2 medium peaches, peeled and sliced
- ½ tsp. sugar
- ½ cup fresh raspberries
- 1 Tbsp. butter
- 3 large eggs, lightly beaten
- ½ cup fat-free milk
- ⅛ tsp. salt
- ½ cup all-purpose flour
- ¼ cup vanilla yogurt

1. Preheat oven to 400°. In a small bowl, toss peaches with sugar; gently stir in raspberries.
2. Place butter in a 9-in. pie plate; heat in oven until butter is melted, 2-3 minutes. Meanwhile, in a small bowl, whisk eggs, milk and salt until blended; gradually whisk in flour. Remove pie plate from oven; tilt carefully to coat bottom and sides with butter. Immediately pour in egg mixture.
3. Bake until pancake is puffed and browned, 18-22 minutes. Remove from oven; serve immediately with fruit and yogurt.
1 SLICE WITH ½ CUP FRUIT AND 1 TBSP. YOGURT: 199 cal., 7g fat (3g sat. fat), 149mg chol., 173mg sod., 25g carb. (11g sugars, 3g fiber), 9g pro. **DIABETIC EXCHANGES:** 1 medium-fat meat, 1 fruit, ½ starch, ½ fat.

CHERRY CHIP SCONES

These buttery scones, dotted with dried cherries and white chips, are so sweet and flaky that sometimes I serve them for dessert. What a treat with hot coffee!
—Pam Brooks, South Berwick, ME

- -

PREP: 15 min. • **BAKE:** 20 min.
MAKES: 8 scones

- 3   cups all-purpose flour
- ½   cup sugar
- 2½ tsp. baking powder
- ½   tsp. baking soda
- 6   Tbsp. cold butter
- 1   cup (8 oz.) vanilla yogurt
- ¼   cup plus 2 Tbsp. whole milk, divided
- 1⅓ cups dried cherries
- ⅔   cup white baking chips
       Coarse sugar, optional

1. Preheat oven to 400°. In a large bowl, combine flour, sugar, baking powder and baking soda. Cut in butter until the mixture resembles coarse crumbs. Combine yogurt and ¼ cup milk; stir into crumb mixture just until moistened. Knead in cherries and chips.
2. On a greased baking sheet, pat dough into a 9-in. circle. Cut into eight wedges; separate wedges. Brush with remaining milk; sprinkle with sugar if desired. Bake until golden brown, 20-25 minutes. Serve warm.
FREEZE OPTION: Freeze cooled scones in freezer containers. To use, thaw desired number of scones at room temperature, or microwave each scone on high until heated through, 20-30 seconds.
1 SCONE: 494 cal., 15g fat (9g sat. fat), 29mg chol., 340mg sod., 83g carb. (44g sugars, 2g fiber), 8g pro.

YOGURT & HONEY
FRUIT CUPS

YOGURT & HONEY FRUIT CUPS

This tasty combo of fresh fruit and creamy orange-kissed yogurt is guaranteed to disappear fast.
—*Taste of Home* Test Kitchen

- -

TAKES: 10 min. • **MAKES:** 6 servings

- 4½ cups cut-up fresh fruit (pears, apples, bananas, grapes, etc.)
- ¾   cup (6 oz.) mandarin orange, vanilla or lemon yogurt
- 1   Tbsp. honey
- ½   tsp. grated orange zest
- ¼   tsp. almond extract

Divide fruit among six individual serving bowls. Combine the yogurt, honey, orange zest and extract; spoon over the fruit.
¾ CUP: 97 cal., 0 fat (0 sat. fat), 2mg chol., 22mg sod., 23g carb. (9g sugars, 2g fiber), 2g pro. **DIABETIC EXCHANGES:** 1 fruit, ½ starch.

SPICY MAPLE SAUSAGES

Wake up your guests' taste buds with this easy treatment for breakfast sausages from our home economists. Just five ingredients are needed for the sweet and spicy glaze.
—*Taste of Home* Test Kitchen

- -

TAKES: 15 min. • **MAKES:** 20 sausages

- 2   pkg. (7 oz. each) frozen fully cooked breakfast sausage links
- ¼   cup maple syrup
- ¼   cup honey
- 2   tsp. Dijon mustard
- ½   tsp. ground cinnamon
- ½   tsp. cayenne pepper

In a large skillet, cook sausage links until browned; drain. Combine the remaining ingredients; stir into skillet. Bring to a boil; cook and stir for 2-3 minutes or until sausages are glazed.
1 SAUSAGE: 102 cal., 8g fat (3g sat. fat), 12mg chol., 202mg sod., 7g carb. (6g sugars, 0 fiber), 3g pro.

FIESTA BREAKFAST BAKE

Whether my family wants breakfast for dinner or I'm organizing a crowd for a cozy weekend brunch, this is the recipe I turn to. I created the dish by combining my family's favorite southwest flavors in an all-in-one-pan recipe.
—Whitney Gilbert, Smithville, MO

- -

PREP: 15 min. • **BAKE:** 35 min.
MAKES: 8 servings

- 1   tube (16.3 oz.) refrigerated corn biscuits
- 3   cups frozen seasoning blend vegetables (about 14 oz.)
- 1½ cups shredded Monterey Jack cheese
- 8   large eggs
- ¾   cup 2% milk
- ⅛   tsp. cayenne pepper
- ¼   tsp. salt
- ¼   tsp. black pepper
- ¼   tsp. ground cumin
- ½   cup salsa
     Fresh cilantro leaves
     Additional salsa

1. Preheat oven to 350°. Cut biscuits into quarters; arrange evenly in a greased 13x9-in. baking dish. Layer with vegetables and shredded cheese. Whisk together eggs, milk and seasonings; pour evenly over the top. Top with salsa.
2. Bake, uncovered, until casserole is browned and middle is set, 35-45 minutes. Let stand 10 minutes before serving. Top individual servings with fresh cilantro and additional salsa.
1 PIECE: 349 cal., 18g fat (8g sat. fat), 207mg chol., 823mg sod., 32g carb. (8g sugars, 2g fiber), 15g pro.

FIESTA BREAKFAST BAKE

HAM & CHEESE OMELET ROLL

This brunch dish has wonderful flavor and an impressive presentation all rolled into one. A platter of these swirled slices disappears in no time.
—Nancy Daugherty, Cortland, OH

- -

PREP: 15 min. • **BAKE:** 35 min.
MAKES: 12 servings

- 4   oz. cream cheese, softened
- ¾   cup 2% milk
- 2   Tbsp. all-purpose flour
- ¼   tsp. salt
- 12 large eggs
- 2   Tbsp. Dijon mustard
- 2¼ cups shredded cheddar cheese, divided
- 2   cups finely chopped fully cooked ham
- ½   cup thinly sliced green onions

1. Line the bottom and sides of a greased 15x10x1-in. baking pan with parchment; grease the paper and set aside.
2. In a small bowl, beat cream cheese and milk until smooth. Add flour and salt; mix until combined. In a large bowl, whisk eggs until blended. Add cream cheese mixture; mix well. Pour into prepared pan.
3. Bake at 375° for 30-35 minutes or until eggs are puffed and set. Remove from the oven. Immediately spread with mustard and sprinkle with 1 cup cheese. Sprinkle with ham, onions and 1 cup cheese.
4. Roll up from a short side, peeling the parchment away while rolling. Sprinkle top of roll with the remaining cheese; bake 3-4 minutes longer or until cheese is melted.
1 SLICE: 239 cal., 17g fat (9g sat. fat), 260mg chol., 637mg sod., 4g carb. (2g sugars, 0 fiber), 17g pro.

OVERNIGHT CINNAMON ROLLS

CRAB QUICHE

Chopped green onions and sweet red pepper bring a bit of color to this golden entree. The creamy filling features imitation crabmeat and Swiss cheese.
—*Taste of Home* Test Kitchen

PREP: 20 min. • **BAKE:** 30 min. + cooling
MAKES: 8 servings

- 1 unbaked pastry shell (9 in.)
- 1 cup shredded Swiss cheese, divided
- ½ cup chopped sweet red pepper
- ¼ cup chopped green onions
- 1 Tbsp. butter
- 3 large eggs
- 1½ cups half-and-half cream
- ½ tsp. salt
- ¼ tsp. pepper
- ¾ cup flaked imitation crabmeat, chopped

1. Line unpricked pastry shell with a double thickness of heavy-duty foil. Bake at 450° for 5 minutes; remove foil. Bake 5 minutes longer. Immediately sprinkle ½ cup cheese over crust.
2. Reduce heat to 375°. In a skillet, saute red pepper and onions in butter until tender.
3. In a large bowl, whisk the eggs, cream, salt and pepper. Stir in crab, red pepper mixture and the remaining cheese. Pour into the crust.
4. Bake for 30-35 minutes or until a knife inserted in the center comes out clean. Let stand 15 minutes before cutting.
1 SLICE: 290 cal., 19g fat (10g sat. fat), 125mg chol., 432mg sod., 18g carb. (4g sugars, 0 fiber), 10g pro.

OVERNIGHT CINNAMON ROLLS

I like to try different fun fillings in these soft rolls, and each one is packed with cinnamon flavor. They are definitely worth the overnight wait.
—Chris O'Connell, San Antonio, TX

PREP: 35 min. + rising • **BAKE:** 20 min.
MAKES: 2 dozen

- 2 pkg. (¼ oz. each) active dry yeast
- 1½ cups warm water (110° to 115°)
- 2 large eggs
- ½ cup butter, softened
- ½ cup sugar
- 2 tsp. salt
- 5¾ to 6¼ cups all-purpose flour

CINNAMON FILLING
- 1 cup packed brown sugar
- 4 tsp. ground cinnamon
- ½ cup softened butter, divided

GLAZE
- 2 cups confectioners' sugar
- ¼ cup half-and-half cream
- 2 tsp. vanilla extract

1. In a small bowl, dissolve yeast in warm water. In a large bowl, combine eggs, butter, sugar, salt, yeast mixture and 3 cups flour; beat on medium speed until smooth. Stir in enough remaining flour to form a very soft dough (dough will be sticky). Do not knead. Cover with plastic wrap; refrigerate overnight.
2. In a small bowl, mix brown sugar and cinnamon. Turn dough onto a floured surface; divide dough in half. Roll one portion into an 18x12-in. rectangle. Spread with ¼ cup butter to within ½ in. of edges; sprinkle evenly with half of the brown sugar mixture.
3. Roll up jelly-roll style, starting with a long side; pinch seam to seal. Cut into 12 slices. Place in a greased 13x9-in. baking pan, cut side down. Repeat with remaining dough and filling.
4. Cover with kitchen towels; let rise in a warm place until doubled, about 1 hour. Preheat oven to 375°.
5. Bake 20-25 minutes or until lightly browned. In a small bowl, mix confectioners' sugar, cream and vanilla; spread over warm rolls.
1 ROLL: 278 cal., 9g fat (5g sat. fat), 39mg chol., 262mg sod., 47g carb. (23g sugars, 1g fiber), 4g pro.

CRAB QUICHE

SWEET & SPICY BACON

Chili powder, cayenne and curry add an unexpected flavor twist to taste-tempting bacon. With a touch of cinnamon and maple syrup, these addictive strips complement just about any breakfast entree.
—*Taste of Home* Test Kitchen

- -

TAKES: 25 min. • **MAKES:** 4 servings

- 1 tsp. chili powder
- ⅛ tsp. cayenne pepper
- ⅛ tsp. curry powder
- ⅛ tsp. ground cinnamon
- 8 bacon strips
- 3 Tbsp. maple syrup

Combine the seasonings; sprinkle over both sides of the bacon. Place on a rack in an ungreased 15x10x1-in. baking pan. Bake at 450° for 10 minutes. Drizzle with 1 Tbsp. syrup. Turn bacon and drizzle with remaining syrup. Bake for 6-10 minutes longer or until browned. Remove to paper towels. Serve bacon warm.

2 PIECES : 115 cal., 6g fat (2g sat. fat), 11mg chol., 210mg sod., 11g carb. (10g sugars, 0 fiber), 4g pro.

LEMON BLUEBERRY DROP SCONES

I enjoy serving these fruity scones at baby and bridal showers. They're a bit lower in fat than other scone recipes, so you can indulge with little guilt.
—Jacqueline Hendershot, Orange, CA

- -

TAKES: 30 min. • **MAKES:** 14 scones

- 2 cups all-purpose flour
- ⅓ cup sugar
- 2 tsp. baking powder
- 1 tsp. grated lemon zest
- ½ tsp. baking soda
- ¼ tsp. salt
- 1 cup lemon yogurt
- 1 large egg
- ¼ cup butter, melted
- 1 cup fresh or frozen blueberries

GLAZE
- ½ cup confectioners' sugar
- 1 Tbsp. lemon juice
- ½ tsp. grated lemon zest

1. In a large bowl, combine the first six ingredients. In another bowl, combine the yogurt, egg and butter. Stir into dry ingredients just until moistened. Fold in the blueberries.

2. Drop by heaping tablespoonfuls 2 in. apart onto a greased baking sheet. Bake at 400° for 15-18 minutes or until lightly browned. Combine glaze ingredients; drizzle over warm scones.

NOTE: If using frozen blueberries, use the berries without thawing to avoid discoloring the batter.

1 SCONE: 158 cal., 4g fat (2g sat. fat), 25mg chol., 192mg sod., 28g carb. (13g sugars, 1g fiber), 3g pro.

LEMON BLUEBERRY DROP SCONES

OAT PANCAKES

RASPBERRY STREUSEL COFFEE CAKE

One of my mother's friends used to bring this over at the holidays, and it never lasted long. With tangy raspberry filling, tender cake and crunchy topping, it has become a favorite at our house.
—Amy Mitchell, Sabetha, KS

PREP: 25 min. + cooling • **BAKE:** 40 min.
MAKES: 16 servings

- 3½ cups unsweetened raspberries
- 1 cup water
- 2 Tbsp. lemon juice
- 1¼ cups sugar
- ⅓ cup cornstarch

BATTER
- 3 cups all-purpose flour
- 1 cup sugar
- 1 tsp. baking powder
- 1 tsp. baking soda
- 1 cup cold butter, cubed
- 2 large eggs, lightly beaten
- 1 cup sour cream
- 1 tsp. vanilla extract

TOPPING
- ½ cup all-purpose flour
- ½ cup sugar
- ¼ cup butter, softened
- ½ cup chopped pecans

GLAZE
- ½ cup confectioners' sugar
- 2 tsp. 2% milk
- ½ tsp. vanilla extract

1. In a large saucepan, cook raspberries and water over medium heat 5 minutes. Add lemon juice. Combine sugar and cornstarch; stir into fruit mixture. Bring to a boil; cook and stir 2 minutes or until thickened. Cool.
2. Preheat oven to 350°. In a large bowl, combine flour, sugar, baking powder and baking soda. Cut in butter until mixture resembles coarse crumbs. Stir in eggs, sour cream and vanilla (batter will be stiff).
3. Spread half into a greased 13x9-in. baking dish. Spread raspberry filling over batter; spoon remaining batter over filling. Combine topping ingredients; sprinkle over top.
4. Bake 40-45 minutes or until golden brown. Combine glaze ingredients; drizzle over warm cake.
1 PIECE: 462 cal., 20g fat (11g sat. fat), 75mg chol., 265mg sod., 65g carb. (39g sugars, 2g fiber), 5g pro.

OAT PANCAKES

My daughter brought this recipe home from school one day, and we loved it. Since then, these pancakes have been a regular part of Sunday morning breakfast, served with maple syrup, flavored syrup or applesauce, and a big helping of grits.
—Linda Hicks, Pinconning, MI

TAKES: 20 min. • **MAKES:** 6 servings

- 1 cup quick-cooking oats
- 1 cup all-purpose flour
- 2 Tbsp. sugar
- 2 tsp. baking powder
- 1 tsp. salt
- 2 large eggs, lightly beaten
- 1½ cups fat-free milk
- ¼ cup canola oil
- 1 tsp. lemon juice

1. In a large bowl, combine the first five ingredients. Combine the eggs, milk, oil and lemon juice; add to dry ingredients and stir just until moistened.
2. Pour batter by ¼ cupfuls onto a lightly greased hot griddle; turn when bubbles form on top of pancakes. Cook until second side is golden brown.
2 PANCAKES: 241 cal., 12g fat (0 sat. fat), 71mg chol., 581mg sod., 25g carb. (0 sugars, 0 fiber), 8g pro. **DIABETIC EXCHANGES:** 1½ starch, 1 fat, ½ fat-free milk.

TEST KITCHEN TIP

In most cases, quick-cooking oats and old-fashioned oats are interchangeable, as long as you consider the differences between the two. Quick-cooking oats cook faster, obviously, but they also offer a more delicate texture to baked goods and desserts. If you want a heartier texture in your items, use old-fashioned oats.

BREAKFAST
SWEET POTATOES

BREAKFAST SWEET POTATOES

Baked sweet potatoes aren't just for dinner anymore. Top them with breakfast favorites to power up your morning.

—*Taste of Home* Test Kitchen

PREP: 10 min. • **BAKE:** 45 min.
MAKES: 4 servings

- 4 medium sweet potatoes (about 8 oz. each)
- ½ cup fat-free coconut Greek yogurt
- 1 medium apple, chopped
- 2 Tbsp. maple syrup
- ¼ cup toasted unsweetened coconut flakes

1. Preheat oven to 400°. Place potatoes on a foil-lined baking sheet. Bake until tender, 45-60 minutes.

2. With a sharp knife, cut an "X" in each potato. Fluff pulp with a fork. Top with remaining ingredients.

1 STUFFED SWEET POTATO: 321 cal., 3g fat (2g sat. fat), 0 chol., 36mg sod., 70g carb. (35g sugars, 8g fiber), 7g pro.

LIGHT & CRISPY WAFFLES

Club soda gives these crisp waffles a light, fluffy texture. With only four ingredients, homemade waffles can't get much easier than this!

—*Taste of Home* Test Kitchen

TAKES: 20 min. • **MAKES:** 12 waffles

- 2 cups biscuit/baking mix
- 2 large eggs, lightly beaten
- ½ cup canola oil
- 1 cup club soda

1. In a large bowl, combine biscuit mix, eggs and oil. Add club soda; stir until smooth.

2. Bake in a preheated waffle iron according to the manufacturer's directions until golden brown.

FREEZE OPTION: Cool waffles on wire racks. Freeze between layers of waxed paper in freezer containers. To use, reheat waffles in a toaster on medium setting. Or, microwave each waffle on high until heated through, 30-60 seconds.

2 WAFFLES: 348 cal., 26g fat (4g sat. fat), 71mg chol., 533mg sod., 25g carb. (1g sugars, 1g fiber), 5g pro.

SPECIAL MORNING POPOVERS

SPECIAL MORNING POPOVERS

Popovers are a Christmas morning tradition my father-in-law started more than 30 years ago. Now I always get up early to make the popovers, then wake the family to begin opening gifts. When the popovers are ready, I serve them with lots of butter and assorted jams.

—Sue Jurack, Mequon, WI

PREP: 15 min. • **BAKE:** 35 min.
MAKES: 9 popovers

- 1¼ cups whole milk
- 1 Tbsp. butter, melted and cooled
- 1 cup all-purpose flour
- ¼ tsp. salt
- 2 large eggs

1. In a small bowl, beat the milk, butter, flour and salt until blended. Add eggs, one at a time, beating well after each addition. Fill buttered popover pans or large custard cups three-fourths full.

2. Bake at 450° for 15 minutes. Reduce heat to 350°; bake until very firm, 20 minutes longer. Remove from the oven and prick each popover with a sharp knife to allow steam to escape. Serve immediately.

1 POPOVER: 99 cal., 4g fat (2g sat. fat), 55mg chol., 109mg sod., 12g carb. (2g sugars, 0 fiber), 4g pro.

FOUR-TOMATO
SALSA, PAGE 41

Snacks & Appetizers

The staff at the *Taste of Home* Test Kitchen loves a good party! Turn here to see which munchies they rely on most. These finger-licking bites are sure to become staples at your get-togethers, too.

TOMATO-ONION
PHYLLO PIZZA

TOMATO-ONION PHYLLO PIZZA

With a delicate crust and lots of lovely tomatoes on top, this dish is a delight to serve guests. I make it often when fresh garden tomatoes are in season. It freezes very well unbaked, so I can keep one on hand to pop in the oven whenever I need a quick appetizer.
—Neta Cohen, Bedford, VA

- -

PREP: 20 min. • **BAKE:** 20 min.
MAKES: 28 slices

- 5 Tbsp. butter, melted
- 14 sheets phyllo dough (14x9 in.)
- 7 Tbsp. grated Parmesan cheese, divided
- 1 cup shredded part-skim mozzarella cheese
- 1 cup thinly sliced onion
- 1 lb. plum tomatoes, sliced
- 1½ tsp. minced fresh oregano or ½ tsp. dried oregano
- 1 tsp. minced fresh thyme or ¼ tsp. dried thyme
  Salt and pepper to taste

1. Brush a 15x10x1-in. baking pan with some of the melted butter. Unroll phyllo dough; cut stack into a 10½x9-in. rectangle. Discard the scraps.
2. Line bottom of prepared pan with two sheets of phyllo dough (sheets will overlap slightly). Brush with butter and sprinkle with 1 Tbsp. Parmesan cheese. Repeat the layers 5 times. (Keep dough covered with plastic wrap and a damp towel until ready to use to prevent it from drying out.)
3. Top with layers of remaining phyllo dough; brush with remaining butter. Sprinkle with mozzarella cheese; arrange the onion and tomatoes over the cheese. Sprinkle with oregano, thyme, salt, pepper and remaining Parmesan cheese. Bake at 375° until edges are golden brown, 20-25 minutes.
1 PIECE: 54 cal., 3g fat (2g sat. fat), 9mg chol., 87mg sod., 4g carb. (1g sugars, 0 fiber), 2g pro.

GRILLED WING ZINGERS

GRILLED WING ZINGERS

My husband fine-tuned this recipe, and the results were spectacular! These spicy-hot grilled wings are true party pleasers. You can easily adjust the heat level by altering the amount of chili powder. The wings take a little time, but they're worth it.
—Angela Roster, Greenbackville, VA

- -

PREP: 35 min. • **GRILL:** 35 min.
MAKES: about 6½ dozen

- 8 lbs. chicken wings
- 1 cup packed brown sugar
- 1 cup Louisiana-style hot sauce
- ¼ cup butter, cubed
- 1 Tbsp. cider vinegar
- ⅓ cup sugar
- ½ cup Italian seasoning
- ¼ cup dried rosemary, crushed
- ¼ cup paprika
- ¼ cup chili powder
- ¼ cup pepper
- 2 Tbsp. cayenne pepper
- 1 cup blue cheese salad dressing
- ½ cup ranch salad dressing
  Celery sticks

1. Cut chicken wings into three sections; discard wing tip sections. Set wings aside.
2. In a small saucepan, bring brown sugar, hot sauce, butter and vinegar to a boil. Reduce heat; simmer, uncovered, until the butter is melted and the sauce is heated through, 6-8 minutes. Cool.
3. In a gallon-size resealable plastic bag, combine sugar and seasonings. Add chicken wings in batches; seal bag and toss to coat pieces evenly.
4. Grill, covered, over indirect medium heat until juices run clear, 35-45 minutes, turning and basting occasionally with sauce.
5. In a small bowl, combine blue cheese and ranch salad dressing; serve with the chicken wings and celery sticks.
NOTE: Uncooked chicken wing sections (wingettes) may be substituted for whole chicken wings.
1 PIECE: 96 cal., 6g fat (2g sat. fat), 18mg chol., 170mg sod., 5g carb. (4g sugars, 1g fiber), 5g pro.

CREAMY PEPPERMINT PATTIES

These smooth chocolate candies fill the bill for hosts who like to add a little sweetness to their appetizer buffets.
—Donna Gonda, North Canton, OH

PREP: 40 min. + chilling
MAKES: about 8 dozen

- 1 pkg. (8 oz.) cream cheese, softened
- 1 tsp. peppermint extract
- 9 cups confectioners' sugar
- 1½ cups milk chocolate chips
- 1½ cups semisweet chocolate chips
- 3 Tbsp. shortening

1. Beat the cream cheese and extract until smooth. Gradually add confectioners' sugar, beating well.

2. Shape into 1-in. balls. Place on waxed paper-lined baking sheets. Flatten into patties 1½-1¾ in. in diameter. Cover and refrigerate until chilled, about 1 hour.

3. In a microwave, melt chips and shortening; stir until smooth. Cool slightly. Dip patties in melted chocolate, allowing excess to drip off; place on waxed paper until set. Store in the refrigerator.

2 PATTIES: 275 cal., 8g fat (4g sat. fat), 12mg chol., 33mg sod., 51g carb. (48g sugars, 0 fiber), 1g pro.

NUTTY STUFFED MUSHROOMS

NUTTY STUFFED MUSHROOMS

Basil, Parmesan cheese and mushroom blend together well, while buttery pecans give these treats unexpected crunch. All of our dear children, grandchildren and great-grandchildren always ask for them!
—Mildred Eldred, Union City, MI

TAKES: 30 min. • **MAKES:** 20 servings

- 20 large fresh mushrooms
- 3 Tbsp. butter
- 1 small onion, chopped
- ¼ cup dry bread crumbs
- ¼ cup finely chopped pecans
- 3 Tbsp. grated Parmesan cheese
- ¼ tsp. salt
- ¼ tsp. dried basil
  Dash cayenne pepper

1. Preheat oven to 400°. Remove stems from mushrooms; set caps aside. Finely chop stems. In a large skillet, heat butter over medium heat. Add the chopped mushrooms and onion; saute until liquid has evaporated, about 5 minutes. Remove from heat; set aside.

2. Meanwhile, combine all the remaining ingredients; add mushroom mixture. Stuff firmly into mushroom caps. Bake the caps, uncovered, in a greased 15x10x1-in. baking pan until tender, 15-18 minutes. Serve warm.

1 STUFFED MUSHROOM: 44 cal., 3g fat (1g sat. fat), 5mg chol., 67mg sod., 3g carb. (0 sugars, 0 fiber), 2g pro.

PEPPERONI STUFFED MUSHROOMS:
Prepare mushroom caps as directed. Omit pecans, salt, basil and pepper. Add 1 minced garlic clove to chopped mushrooms and onion when sauteing. Stir into mushroom mixture bread crumbs, Parmesan cheese, 3 oz. finely chopped pepperoni, 1 Tbsp. minced parsley and ⅛ tsp. pepper. Bake at 375° until tender, 15-20 minutes. Serve warm.

SOFT BEER PRETZELS

I'm always looking for new ways to combine fun flavors, and what goes together better than beer and pretzels? Not much that I can think of. That's why I put them together in one delicious recipe.
—Alyssa Wilhite, Whitehouse, TX

PREP: 1 hour + rising • **BAKE:** 10 min.
MAKES: 8 pretzels

- 1 bottle (12 oz.) amber beer or nonalcoholic beer
- 1 pkg. (¼ oz.) active dry yeast
- 2 Tbsp. unsalted butter, melted
- 2 Tbsp. sugar
- 1½ tsp. salt
- 4 to 4½ cups all-purpose flour
- 10 cups water
- ⅔ cup baking soda

TOPPING

- 1 large egg yolk
- 1 Tbsp. water
  Coarse salt, optional

1. In a small saucepan, heat the beer to 110°-115°; remove from heat. Stir in yeast until dissolved. In a large bowl, combine butter, sugar, 1½ tsp. salt, yeast mixture and 3 cups flour; beat on medium speed until smooth. Stir in enough remaining flour to form a soft dough (dough will be sticky).

2. Turn dough onto a floured surface; knead until smooth and elastic, about 6-8 minutes. Place in a greased bowl, turning once to grease the top. Cover with plastic wrap and let rise in a warm place until doubled, about 1 hour.

3. Preheat oven to 425°. Punch dough down. Turn onto a lightly floured surface; divide and shape into eight balls. Roll each into a 24-in. rope. Curve ends of each rope to form a circle; twist the ends once and lay over opposite side of circle, pinching ends to seal.

4. In a Dutch oven, bring water and baking soda to a boil. Carefully drop pretzels, two at a time, into boiling water. Cook 30 seconds. Remove with a slotted spoon; drain well on paper towels.

5. Place 2 in. apart on greased baking sheets. In a small bowl, whisk egg yolk and water; brush over pretzels. Sprinkle with coarse salt if desired. Bake until golden brown, 10-12 minutes. Carefully remove from pans to a wire rack to cool.

FREEZE OPTION: Freeze cooled pretzels in resealable plastic freezer bags. To use, thaw pretzels at room temperature or, if desired, microwave each one on high until heated through, 20-30 seconds.

1 PRETZEL: 288 cal., 4g fat (2g sat. fat), 16mg chol., 604mg sod., 53g carb. (6g sugars, 2g fiber), 7g pro.

TO MAKE PRETZEL BITES: Divide and shape into eight balls; roll each into a 12-in. rope. Cut each rope into 1-in. pieces. Boil and top as directed; bake at 400° until golden brown, 6-8 minutes.

STRAWBERRY MIMOSAS

Here's a tasty twist on the classic mimosa. To make this refreshing drink friendly for kids or mamas-to-be, substitute lemon-lime soda or ginger ale for the champagne.
—Kelly Maxwell, Plainfield, IL

TAKES: 15 min.
MAKES: 12 servings (1 cup each)

- 7 cups sliced fresh strawberries (about 2 qt.)
- 3 cups orange juice
- 4 cups champagne, chilled

GARNISHES

  Fresh strawberries and orange slices, optional

1. Place half of the strawberries and orange juice in a blender; cover and process until smooth. Press through a fine mesh strainer. Repeat with the remaining strawberries and orange juice.

2. Pour a scant ⅔ cup strawberry mixture into each champagne flute or wine glass. Top with about ⅓ cup champagne. If desired, serve with a strawberry and an orange slice.

1 CUP: 121 cal., 0 fat (0 sat. fat), 0 chol., 7mg sod., 16g carb. (10g sugars, 2g fiber), 1g pro.

SOFT BEER PRETZELS

ONION BRIE APPETIZERS

3. Roll up one long side to the middle of the dough; roll up the other side so the two rolls meet in the center. Using a serrated knife, cut into ½-in. slices. Place on parchment-lined baking sheets; flatten slices to ¼-in. thickness. Refrigerate for 15 minutes.

4. In a small bowl, beat egg and water; brush over slices. Bake at 375° until puffed and golden brown, 12-14 minutes. Serve warm.

1 SERVING: 121 cal., 8g fat (3g sat. fat), 23mg chol., 109mg sod., 11g carb. (3g sugars, 1g fiber), 3g pro.

SAVORY PARTY BREAD

It's impossible to stop nibbling on warm pieces of this cheesy, oniony loaf. The bread fans out for an impressive presentation.
—Kay Daly, Raleigh, NC

- -

PREP: 10 min. • **BAKE:** 25 min.
MAKES: 8 servings

    1   unsliced round loaf
        sourdough bread (1 lb.)
    1   lb. Monterey Jack cheese
    ½   cup butter, melted
    ½   cup chopped green onions
    2   to 3 tsp. poppy seeds

1. Preheat oven to 350°. Cut the bread widthwise into 1-in. slices to within ½ in. of bottom of loaf. Repeat cuts in opposite direction. Cut cheese into ¼-in. slices; cut slices into small pieces. Place cheese in cuts.

2. In a small bowl, mix butter, green onions and poppy seeds; drizzle over bread. Wrap in foil; place on a baking sheet. Bake loaf for 15 minutes. Unwrap; bake until cheese is melted, 10 minutes longer.

1 SERVING: 481 cal., 31g fat (17g sat. fat), 91mg chol., 782mg sod., 32g carb. (1g sugars, 2g fiber), 17g pro.

TEST KITCHEN TIP
The bread can be sliced and filled a day ahead. Right before company comes, drizzle the butter, green onions and poppy seeds and bake.

ONION BRIE APPETIZERS

Guests will think you spent hours preparing these cute appetizers, but they're really easy to assemble when you use purchased puff pastry. The tasty combination of Brie, caramelized onions and caraway is terrific.
—Carole Resnick, Cleveland, OH

- -

PREP: 25 min. + chilling • **BAKE:** 15 min.
MAKES: 1½ dozen

    2   medium onions, thinly sliced
    3   Tbsp. butter
    2   Tbsp. brown sugar
    ½   tsp. white wine vinegar
    1   sheet frozen puff pastry, thawed

    4   oz. Brie cheese, rind
        removed, softened
    1   to 2 tsp. caraway seeds
    1   large egg
    2   tsp. water

1. In a large skillet, cook the onions, butter, brown sugar and vinegar over medium-low heat until onions are golden brown, stirring frequently. Remove with a slotted spoon; cool to room temperature.

2. On a lightly floured surface, roll the puff pastry into an 11x8-in. rectangle. Cut Brie into thin slices; distribute evenly over pastry. Cover with the onions; sprinkle with the caraway seeds.

LAYERED ASIAN DIP

Here's a tasty change of pace from the taco spreads and other layered dips you come across at parties. My family loves its tender chunks of chicken and overall Asian flair.
—Bonnie Mazur, Reedsburg, WI

PREP: 20 min. + chilling • **MAKES:** 20 servings

- 1 cup chopped cooked chicken breast
- ½ cup shredded carrot
- ¼ cup chopped unsalted peanuts
- 3 Tbsp. chopped green onions
- 1 Tbsp. minced fresh parsley
- 1 tsp. toasted sesame seeds
- 3 Tbsp. reduced-sodium soy sauce, divided
- 1 garlic clove, minced
- 1½ tsp. cornstarch
- ½ cup water
- 2 Tbsp. brown sugar
- 2 Tbsp. ketchup
- 1½ tsp. Worcestershire sauce
- ½ tsp. cider vinegar
- 2 drops hot pepper sauce
- 1 pkg. (8 oz.) reduced-fat cream cheese
  Assorted rice crackers

1. In a bowl, combine first six ingredients. Mix 2 Tbsp. soy sauce and garlic; toss with the chicken mixture. Refrigerate, covered, several hours.

2. For sauce, in a small saucepan, mix the cornstarch and water until smooth; stir in the brown sugar, ketchup, Worcestershire sauce, vinegar and pepper sauce. Bring to a boil; cook and stir the sauce until thickened, 1-2 minutes. Cool slightly. Refrigerate, covered, until cold.

3. To serve, mix cream cheese and remaining soy sauce until blended; transfer to a serving plate, spreading evenly. Top with chicken mixture. Drizzle with the sauce. Serve with assorted crackers.

1 SERVING: 61 cal., 4g fat (2g sat. fat), 13mg chol., 165mg sod., 3g carb. (2g sugars, 0 fiber), 4g pro. **DIABETIC EXCHANGES:** 1 fat.

MOCHA PUNCH

I first tried this smooth, creamy punch at a friend's Christmas open house. It was so special and distinctive I didn't leave until I had the recipe. Having a frosty glass of this almost decadent chocolate punch feels like sipping a milkshake.
—Yvonne Hatfield, Norman, OK

PREP: 15 min. + chilling
MAKES: 25 servings (¾ cup each)

- 6 cups water
- ½ cup sugar
- ½ cup instant chocolate drink mix
- ¼ cup instant coffee granules
- ½ gallon vanilla ice cream
- ½ gallon chocolate ice cream
- 1 cup heavy whipping cream, whipped

1. In a large saucepan, bring water to a boil. Remove from heat. Add sugar, drink mix and coffee; stir until dissolved. Refrigerate, covered, 4 hours or overnight.

2. About 30 minutes before serving, pour mixture into a large punch bowl. Add scoops of ice cream; stir until partially melted. Top servings with whipped cream.

¾ CUP: 254 cal., 13g fat (8g sat. fat), 46mg chol., 87mg sod., 34g carb. (30g sugars, 1g fiber), 4g pro..

LAYERED
ASIAN DIP

PEPPER POPPERS

These creamy stuffed jalapenos have some bite. They may be the most popular treats I make! My husband is always hinting that I should make a batch.
—Lisa Byington, Johnson City, NY

PREP: 15 min. • **BAKE:** 25 min.
MAKES: about 2 dozen

- 1 pkg. (8 oz.) cream cheese, softened
- 1 cup shredded sharp cheddar cheese
- 1 cup shredded Monterey Jack cheese
- 6 bacon strips, cooked and crumbled
- ¼ tsp. salt
- ¼ tsp. garlic powder
- ¼ tsp. chili powder
- 1 lb. fresh jalapenos, halved lengthwise and seeded
- ½ cup dry bread crumbs
  Sour cream, onion dip or ranch salad dressing

1. In a large bowl, combine the cheeses, bacon and seasonings; mix well. Spoon about 2 tablespoonfuls into each pepper half. Roll in bread crumbs.

2. Place in a greased 15x10x1-in. baking pan. Bake, uncovered, at 325° for 15 minutes for spicy flavor, 25 minutes for medium and 35 minutes for mild. Serve with sour cream, dip or dressing.

NOTE: Wear disposable gloves when cutting hot peppers; the oils can burn skin. Avoid touching your face.

3 POPPERS: 273 cal., 21g fat (13g sat. fat), 63mg chol., 454mg sod., 10g carb. (1g sugars, 2g fiber), 12g pro.

ANTIPASTO APPETIZER SALAD

ANTIPASTO APPETIZER SALAD

Serve this popular dish with a slotted spoon as an appetizer or over torn lettuce or mixed greens to enjoy as a salad. I like to pass along toasted baguette slices on the side.
—Tamra Duncan, Lincoln, AR

PREP: 10 min. + chilling • **MAKES:** 6 cups

- 1 jar (16 oz.) roasted sweet red pepper strips, drained
- ½ lb. part-skim mozzarella cheese, cubed
- 1 cup grape tomatoes
- 1 jar (7½ oz.) marinated quartered artichoke hearts, undrained
- 1 jar (7 oz.) pimiento-stuffed olives, drained
- 1 can (6 oz.) pitted ripe olives, drained
- 1 tsp. dried basil
- 1 tsp. dried parsley flakes
  Pepper to taste
  Toasted baguette slices or romaine lettuce, torn

1. In a large bowl, combine the first nine ingredients; toss to coat. Cover the mixture and refrigerate for at least 4 hours before serving the antipasto.

2. Serve with baguette slices or over lettuce.

NOTE: This recipe was tested with Vlasic roasted red pepper strips.

½ CUP: 132 cal., 11g fat (3g sat. fat), 15mg chol., 651mg sod., 6g carb. (2g sugars, 1g fiber), 4g pro.

READER RAVE

"I substituted fresh red and green peppers and the results were great! Thanks, Tamra, for a super elegant salad."
—GOLLIWOG, TASTEOFHOME.COM

FOUR-TOMATO
SALSA

FOUR-TOMATO SALSA

A variety of tomatoes, onions and peppers makes this chunky salsa so good. Whenever I want to take a batch to a get-together, it's hard to keep my family from finishing it off first, so I sometimes double the recipe.
—Connie Siese, Wayne, MI

- -

TAKES: 20 min. • **MAKES:** 14 cups

- 7 plum tomatoes, chopped
- 7 medium red tomatoes, chopped
- 3 medium yellow tomatoes, chopped
- 3 medium orange tomatoes, chopped
- 1 tsp. salt
- 2 Tbsp. lime juice
- 2 Tbsp. olive oil
- 1 medium white onion, chopped
- 1 medium red onion, chopped
- 2 green onions, chopped
- ½ cup each chopped green, sweet red, orange and yellow pepper
- 3 pepperoncini, chopped
- ⅓ cup mild pickled pepper rings, chopped
- ½ cup minced fresh parsley
- 2 Tbsp. minced fresh cilantro
- 1 Tbsp. dried chervil
    Tortilla chips

1. In a colander, combine the tomatoes and salt. Let drain for 10 minutes.
2. Transfer to a large bowl. Stir in the lime juice, oil, onions, peppers, parsley, cilantro and chervil. Serve salsa with tortilla chips. Refrigerate leftovers for up to 1 week.
NOTE: Look for pepperoncini (pickled peppers) in the pickle and olive section of your grocery store.
¼ CUP: 15 cal., 1g fat (0 sat. fat), 0 chol., 62mg sod., 2g carb. (1g sugars, 1g fiber), 0 pro. **DIABETIC EXCHANGES:** 1 free food.

THREE-CHIP ENGLISH TOFFEE

THREE-CHIP ENGLISH TOFFEE

With its melt-in-your-mouth texture and scrumptiously rich flavor, this is the ultimate toffee! Three different kinds of melted chips, along with a sprinkling of walnuts, top the toffee base. Package these pretty pieces in colorful tins for gifts friends will love.
—Lana Petfield, Richmond, VA

- -

PREP: 15 min. + chilling • **COOK:** 30 min.
MAKES: 20 pieces (about 2½ lbs.)

- ½ tsp. plus 2 cups butter, divided
- 2 cups sugar
- 1 cup slivered almonds
- 1 cup milk chocolate chips
- 1 cup chopped walnuts
- ½ cup semisweet chocolate chips
- ½ cup white baking chips
- 1½ tsp. shortening

1. Butter a 15x10x1-in. pan with ½ tsp. butter. In a heavy saucepan over medium-low heat, bring sugar and remaining butter to a boil, stirring constantly. Cover and cook for 2-3 minutes.
2. Uncover; add almonds. Cook and stir with a clean spoon until a candy thermometer reads 300° (hard-crack stage) and mixture is golden brown.
3. Pour into prepared pan (do not scrape sides of saucepan). Surface will be buttery. Cool for 1-2 minutes. Sprinkle with milk chocolate chips. Let stand for 1-2 minutes; spread chocolate over the top. Sprinkle with walnuts; press down gently with the back of a spoon. Chill for 10 minutes.
4. In a microwave, melt semisweet chips; stir until smooth. Drizzle over the walnuts. Refrigerate for 10 minutes. Melt vanilla chips and shortening; stir until smooth. Drizzle over walnuts. Cover toffee and refrigerate for 1-2 hours. Break into pieces.
1 PIECE: 397 cal., 30g fat (15g sat. fat), 52mg chol., 197mg sod., 32g carb. (26g sugars, 1g fiber), 4g pro.

CUBAN SLIDERS,
PAGE 51

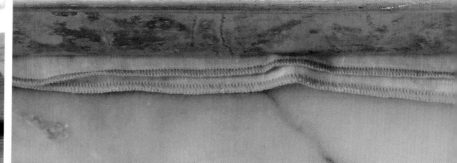

Soups, Salads & Sandwiches

If you're anything like our Test Kitchen pros, you just can't get enough of the classic combo of soup, salad and sammie. Here, our staffers share the favorites they turn to for quick entrees, menu add-ons and potluck contributions alike.

FAVORITE BAKED
POTATO SOUP

FAVORITE BAKED POTATO SOUP

My husband and I enjoyed a delicious potato soup at a restaurant while on vacation, and I came home determined to duplicate it. It took me five years to get the flavor right, but now it's a staple at our house.
—Joann Goetz, Genoa, OH

- -

PREP: 20 min. • **BAKE:** 65 min. + cooling
MAKES: 10 servings

- 4 large baking potatoes (about 12 oz. each)
- ⅔ cup butter, cubed
- ⅔ cup all-purpose flour
- ¾ tsp. salt
- ¼ tsp. white pepper
- 6 cups 2% milk
- 1 cup sour cream
- ¼ cup thinly sliced green onions
- 1 cup shredded cheddar cheese
- 10 bacon strips, cooked and crumbled

1. Preheat oven to 350°. Pierce potatoes several times with a fork; place on a baking sheet. Bake until tender, 65-75 minutes. Cool completely.

2. Peel and cube the potatoes. In a large saucepan, melt butter over medium heat. Stir in flour, salt and pepper until smooth; gradually whisk in milk. Bring to a boil, stirring constantly; cook and stir until thickened, about 2 minutes. Stir in potatoes; heat through.

3. Remove from heat; stir in sour cream and green onions. Top individual servings with cheese and bacon.

1 CUP: 469 cal., 28g fat (17g sat. fat), 86mg chol., 563mg sod., 41g carb. (10g sugars, 3g fiber), 14g pro.

TEST KITCHEN TIP
Real bacon bits work fine for the garnish if you don't have time to cook bacon.

REUBEN SALAD IN A JAR

REUBEN SALAD IN A JAR

Amy Smith from Avon, Connecticut, shared her layered Reuben salad with us, and we couldn't resist making it extra portable. Get ready to be asked for the recipe.
—*Taste of Home* Test Kitchen

- -

TAKES: 30 min. • **MAKES:** 4 servings

- 2 Tbsp. butter, melted
- ⅛ tsp. pepper
- 2 cups cubed rye bread
- ¾ cup Thousand Island salad dressing
- 2 cups chopped pastrami
- 1 cup sauerkraut, rinsed and well drained
- 1 large tomato, diced
- 8 green onions, thinly sliced
- 1 cup shredded Swiss cheese
- 1 pkg. (6 oz.) ready-to-serve salad greens

1. In a bowl, combine butter and pepper. Add bread cubes and toss to coat. Arrange in a single layer in an ungreased 15x10x1-in. baking pan. Bake at 400° until golden brown, 8-10 minutes, stirring occasionally. Cool.

2. In each of four 1-qt. wide-mouth canning jars, divide and layer ingredients in the following order: salad dressing, pastrami, sauerkraut, tomato, green onions, cheese and salad greens. Cover and refrigerate until serving. Divide croutons among 4-oz. glass jars or other small containers; cover. To serve, transfer salads and croutons into bowls; toss to combine.

1 SERVING: 509 cal., 35g fat (13g sat. fat), 81mg chol., 1454mg sod., 24g carb. (10g sugars, 4g fiber), 24g pro.

RANCH CHICKEN SALAD

Serving salad for dinner is anything but skimpy with this recipe. There's chicken and cheese in every bite, and celery and apples give it a pleasing crunch.
—*Taste of Home* Test Kitchen

- -

TAKES: 30 min. • **MAKES:** 4 servings

- 2 Tbsp. plus 1 tsp. paprika
- 4 tsp. brown sugar
- 3 tsp. garlic powder
- 1 tsp. seasoned salt
- ⅛ tsp. cayenne pepper
- 4 boneless skinless chicken breast halves (4 oz. each)
- 2 pkg. (5 oz. each) spring mix salad greens
- 1 cup chopped celery
- 1 cup shredded carrots
- 1 medium apple, chopped
- ½ cup shredded cheddar cheese
- ½ cup reduced-fat ranch salad dressing

1. In a shallow dish, combine the first five ingredients. Add chicken, one piece at a time, and turn to coat. Place chicken on a greased broiler pan. Broil 6 in. from the heat for 6-8 minutes on each side or until chicken juices run clear.

2. Meanwhile, divide salad greens among four dinner plates. Top each with celery, carrots, apple and cheese. Cut chicken into strips; arrange over salads. Drizzle with ranch dressing.

3 CUPS: 320 cal., 14g fat (4g sat. fat), 86mg chol., 784mg sod., 20g carb. (11g sugars, 5g fiber), 29g pro.

SWEET-SOUR
PASTA SALAD

- -

READER RAVE

"Since I first made this, it has been on the menu about every other week! Easy to make and just delicious!"

—LMS803, TASTEOFHOME.COM

- -

SWEET-SOUR PASTA SALAD

A tangy dressing tops off this veggie-filled pasta salad that's actually good for you!
—*Taste of Home* Test Kitchen

- -

PREP: 15 min. + chilling • **COOK:** 15 min.
MAKES: 12 servings (¾ cup each)

- 8 oz. uncooked fusilli or other spiral pasta
- 1 medium zucchini, julienned
- 1 cup fresh cauliflower florets
- 1 cup cherry tomatoes, halved
- 1 small green pepper, chopped
- ½ cup chopped red onion
- 1 cup colossal ripe olives, halved
- ¾ cup pimiento-stuffed olives

DRESSING

- ¼ cup ketchup
- 2 Tbsp. sugar
- 2 Tbsp. white vinegar
- 1 garlic clove, peeled
- 1 tsp. paprika
- ¼ tsp. salt
- ½ small onion, cut into wedges
- ¼ cup canola oil

1. Cook pasta according to package directions. Drain; rinse with cold water and drain well. Transfer to a large bowl. Add vegetables and olives.

2. Place first seven dressing ingredients in a blender; cover and process until blended. While processing, gradually add oil in a steady stream; process until thickened. Add to salad; toss to coat. Refrigerate, covered, at least 2 hours before serving.

¾ CUP: 162 cal., 7g fat (1g sat. fat), 0 chol., 380mg sod., 22g carb. (6g sugars, 2g fiber), 3g pro. **DIABETIC EXCHANGES:** 1½ starch, 1 fat.

MARTY'S BEAN BURGER CHILI

My husband and I met while working the dinner shift at a homeless shelter where they served my chili. I've revised the chili to use bean veggie burgers.
—Marty Nickerson, Ellington, CT

- -

PREP: 15 min. • **COOK:** 7 hours
MAKES: 6 servings

- 2 cans (14½ oz. each) no-salt-added diced tomatoes, drained
- 1 can (14½ oz.) diced tomatoes, drained
- 1 can (16 oz.) kidney beans, undrained
- 1 can (15 oz.) black beans, undrained
- 1 can (15 oz.) garbanzo beans or chickpeas, rinsed and drained
- 4 frozen spicy black bean veggie burgers, thawed and coarsely chopped
- 1 large onion, finely chopped
- 1 large sweet red or green pepper, chopped
- 2 Tbsp. chili powder
- 1 Tbsp. Worcestershire sauce
- 3 tsp. dried basil
- 3 tsp. dried oregano
- 2 tsp. hot pepper sauce
- 2 garlic cloves, minced

Place all ingredients in a 5- or 6-qt. slow cooker; stir to combine. Cook, covered, on low 7-9 hours to allow flavors to blend.

1½ CUPS: 348 cal., 6g fat (0 sat. fat), 0 chol., 1151mg sod., 58g carb. (14g sugars, 19g fiber), 21g pro.

SPINACH PO'BOY

I like to make this warm and cheesy sandwich for a simple dinner, served with fresh fruit on the side.
—Jan Briggs, Greenfield, WI

- -

PREP: 10 min. • **BAKE:** 25 min.
MAKES: 4 servings

- 1 loaf (8 oz.) unsliced French bread
- ½ cup butter, divided
- ⅓ cup chopped green onions
- 6 cups fresh spinach, coarsely chopped
- ½ tsp. garlic powder
- ⅛ tsp. hot pepper sauce
- ½ cup shredded sharp cheddar cheese
- ½ cup shredded mozzarella cheese

1. Cut bread in half lengthwise; spread cut sides with half of the butter. Set aside.
2. In a large skillet, cook onions in remaining butter over medium heat for 4-5 minutes
or until tender. Add the spinach, garlic powder and hot pepper sauce; cook and stir 3 minutes longer or until spinach is tender.
3. Spread over bottom half of loaf; sprinkle with cheeses. Replace bread top. Wrap in foil; place on a baking sheet. Bake at 375° for 20 minutes. Open foil; bake 5 minutes longer or until golden brown. Cut loaf into pieces.

¼ LOAF: 471 cal., 32g fat (19g sat. fat), 86mg chol., 742mg sod., 33g carb. (3g sugars, 2g fiber), 14g pro.

MARTY'S BEAN
BURGER CHILI

¼ tsp. pepper
4 oz. crumbled blue cheese

Place all the ingredients in a blender; cover and process until smooth. Store in the refrigerator.

2 TBSP.: 172 cal., 18g fat (4g sat. fat), 17mg chol., 220mg sod., 1g carb. (0 sugars, 0 fiber), 1g pro.

BLUE CHEESE BACON DRESSING: After processing the dressing, stir in six crumbled cooked bacon strips. Makes 3¼ cups.

TROPICAL SNAP PEA & MANGO SALAD

We toss romaine with chunks of mango, avocado, sugar snap peas and red onion in a homemade honey-lime dressing. A little toasted coconut sprinkled on top adds extra texture.
—*Taste of Home* Test Kitchen

- -

TAKES: 25 min. • **MAKES:** 6 servings

3 cups torn romaine
1½ cups fresh sugar snap peas, trimmed
1 medium mango, peeled and cubed
1 medium ripe avocado, peeled and cubed
½ cup thinly sliced red onion
DRESSING
3 Tbsp. honey
1 tsp. grated lime zest
2 Tbsp. lime juice
1 Tbsp. canola oil
½ cup sweetened shredded coconut, toasted

In a large bowl, combine the first five ingredients. In a small bowl, whisk honey, lime zest, lime juice and oil until blended. Drizzle over salad and toss to coat. Sprinkle with coconut. Serve immediately.

NOTE: To toast coconut, bake in a shallow pan in a 350° oven for 5-10 minutes or cook in a skillet over low heat until golden brown, stirring occasionally.

1 CUP: 191 cal., 10g fat (3g sat. fat), 0 chol., 28mg sod., 26g carb. (19g sugars, 5g fiber), 3g pro.

SPICY FRENCH DIP

SPICY FRENCH DIP

If I'm cooking for a party or family reunion, I can put this beef in the slow cooker in the morning and then concentrate on other preparations. It's a time-saver that never fails to get rave reviews.
—Ginny Koeppen, Winnfield, LA

- -

PREP: 10 min. • **COOK:** 8 hours
MAKES: 12 servings

1 beef sirloin tip roast (3 lbs.), cut in half
½ cup water
1 can (4 oz.) diced jalapeno peppers, drained
1 envelope Italian salad dressing mix
12 crusty rolls (5 in.)

1. Place beef in a 5-qt. slow cooker. In a small bowl, combine the water, jalapenos and dressing mix; pour over beef. Cover and cook on low for 8-10 hours or until meat is tender.

2. Remove beef and shred with two forks. Skim fat from cooking juices. Serve beef on rolls with juice.

1 SANDWICH: 315 cal., 8g fat (2g sat. fat), 72mg chol., 582mg sod., 31g carb. (2g sugars, 1g fiber), 28g pro. **DIABETIC EXCHANGES:** 3 lean meat, 2 starch.

BLUE CHEESE SALAD DRESSING

Here's a terrific finishing touch for any combination of greens. At our house, the thick and creamy salad dressing does double duty as dip for veggies.
—Christy Freeman, Central Point, OR

- -

TAKES: 10 min. • **MAKES:** 3 cups

2 cups mayonnaise
1 cup sour cream
¼ cup white wine vinegar
¼ cup minced fresh parsley
1 garlic clove, crushed
½ tsp. ground mustard
½ tsp. salt

TROPICAL
SNAP PEA
& MANGO
SALAD

MUSHROOM CRAB MELTS

I received this recipe from my grandmother. The rich open-faced treats are a favorite main dish alongside a green salad, but I've also cut them into quarters to serve as hors d'oeuvres. To save time, make the crab-mushroom topping early in the day and store it in the fridge.
—Jean Bevilacqua, Rhododendron, OR

TAKES: 30 min. • **MAKES:** 6 servings

- 3   bacon strips, diced
- 1   cup sliced fresh mushrooms
- ¼   cup chopped onion
- 1   can (6 oz.) crabmeat, drained, flaked and cartilage removed or 1 cup chopped imitation crabmeat
- 1   cup shredded Swiss cheese
- ½   cup mayonnaise
- ⅓   cup grated Parmesan cheese
- 2   Tbsp. butter, softened
- 6   English muffins, split
     Dash each cayenne pepper and paprika

1. Preheat oven to 400°. In a large skillet, cook bacon over medium heat until crisp; remove to paper towels. Drain drippings from skillet, reserving 2 Tbsp. Saute mushrooms and onion in drippings until tender.
2. In a large bowl, combine crab, Swiss cheese, mayonnaise, mushroom mixture, Parmesan cheese and bacon.
3. Spread butter over muffin halves. Top with crab mixture; sprinkle with cayenne and paprika. Place on an ungreased baking sheet.
4. Bake until lightly browned, 10-15 minutes.
1 SERVING: 485 cal., 33g fat (11g sat. fat), 70mg chol., 710mg sod., 28g carb. (3g sugars, 2g fiber), 19g pro.

ITALIAN SAUSAGE KALE SOUP

My mother dehydrates the last pick of tomatoes from her garden each fall, and they're perfect for quick soups like this. If I don't have time to prepare dry beans, canned beans work just as well.
—Lori Terry, Chicago, IL

PREP: 15 min. • **COOK:** 20 min.
MAKES: 8 servings (2 qt.)

- 1   pkg. (19½ oz.) Italian turkey sausage links, casings removed
- 1   medium onion, chopped
- 8   cups chopped fresh kale
- 2   garlic cloves, minced
- ¼   tsp. crushed red pepper flakes, optional
- ½   cup white wine or chicken stock
- 3¾ cups chicken stock (26 oz.)
- 1   can (15 oz.) cannellini beans, rinsed and drained
- 1   can (14½ oz.) no-salt-added diced tomatoes, undrained
- ½   cup sun-dried tomatoes (not packed in oil), chopped
- ¼   tsp. pepper

1. In a 6-qt. stockpot, cook sausage and onion over medium heat 6-8 minutes or until no longer pink, breaking into crumbles. Remove with a slotted spoon.
2. Add kale to the pot; cook and stir for 2 minutes. Add garlic and, if desired, red pepper flakes; cook 1 minute. Add wine; cook 2 minutes longer.
3. Stir in sausage mixture and remaining ingredients. Bring to a boil. Reduce heat; simmer, covered, 15-20 minutes or until kale is tender.
1 CUP: 217 cal., 8g fat (2g sat. fat), 51mg chol., 868mg sod., 15g carb. (5g sugars, 4g fiber), 18g pro.

ITALIAN SAUSAGE
KALE SOUP

CUBAN SLIDERS

CREAMY WHITE CHILI

Years ago, as a time-starved college student, I got this wonderful recipe from my sister-in-law, who made a big batch and served it to a crowd one night. It was a hit—and easy and quick. In all my years of cooking, I've never had another dish get so many compliments.
—Laura Brewer, Lafayette, IN

- -

PREP: 10 min. • **COOK:** 40 min.
MAKES: 7 servings

- 1 lb. boneless skinless chicken breasts, cut into ½-in. cubes
- 1 medium onion, chopped
- 1½ tsp. garlic powder
- 1 Tbsp. canola oil
- 2 cans (15½ oz. each) great northern beans, rinsed and drained
- 1 can (14½ oz.) chicken broth
- 2 cans (4 oz. each) chopped green chiles
- 1 tsp. salt
- 1 tsp. ground cumin
- 1 tsp. dried oregano
- ½ tsp. pepper
- ¼ tsp. cayenne pepper
- 1 cup sour cream
- ½ cup heavy whipping cream
  Tortilla chips, optional
  Shredded cheddar cheese, optional
  Sliced seeded jalapeno pepper, optional

1. In a large saucepan, saute the chicken, onion and garlic powder in oil until chicken is no longer pink. Add the beans, broth, chiles and seasonings. Bring to a boil. Reduce heat; simmer, uncovered, for 30 minutes.
2. Remove from the heat; stir in sour cream and cream. If desired, top with tortilla chips, cheese and jalapenos.
1 CUP: 334 cal., 16g fat (8g sat. fat), 81mg chol., 1045mg sod., 24g carb. (3g sugars, 7g fiber), 22g pro.

> **TEST KITCHEN TIP**
> You can make this using half-and-half cream instead of heavy cream if that's what you have on hand.

CUBAN SLIDERS

Followers of my blog, houseofyumm.com, go nuts for these. Bake the wonderful little rolls until they are lightly toasted and the cheese melts. The leftovers keep really well in the fridge, and they make a lovely cold snack or quick lunch.
—Serene Herrera, Dallas, TX

- -

TAKES: 30 min. • **MAKES:** 2 dozen

- 2 pkg. (12 oz. each) Hawaiian sweet rolls
- 1¼ lbs. thinly sliced deli ham
- 9 slices Swiss cheese (about 6 oz.)
- 24 dill pickle slices
TOPPING
- ½ cup butter, cubed
- 2 Tbsp. finely chopped onion
- 2 Tbsp. Dijon mustard

1. Preheat oven to 350°. Without separating the rolls, cut each package of rolls in half horizontally; arrange bottom halves in a greased 13x9-in. baking pan. Layer with ham, cheese and pickles; replace the top halves of rolls.
2. In a microwave, melt butter; stir in the onion and mustard. Drizzle over the rolls. Bake, covered, 10 minutes. Uncover; bake until golden brown and heated through, 5-10 minutes longer.
2 SLIDERS: 382 cal., 19g fat (11g sat. fat), 84mg chol., 1065mg sod., 34g carb. (12g sugars, 2g fiber), 19g pro.

BROCCOLI
BEER CHEESE
SOUP

BROCCOLI BEER CHEESE SOUP

Whether you include the beer or not, this soup tastes wonderful. I always make extra and pop individual servings into the freezer.
—Lori Lee, Brooksville, FL

- -

PREP: 20 min. • **COOK:** 30 min.
MAKES: 10 servings (2½ qt.)

- 3 Tbsp. butter
- 5 celery ribs, finely chopped
- 3 medium carrots, finely chopped
- 1 small onion, finely chopped
- 4 cups fresh broccoli florets, chopped
- ¼ cup chopped sweet red pepper
- 4 cans (14½ oz. each) chicken broth
- ½ tsp. pepper
- ½ cup all-purpose flour
- ½ cup water
- 3 cups shredded cheddar cheese
- 1 pkg. (8 oz.) cream cheese, cubed
- 1 bottle (12 oz.) beer or nonalcoholic beer
  Additional shredded cheddar cheese, optional
  Bacon strips, cooked and crumbled, optional
  Chopped green onions, optional
  Sour cream, optional
  Salad croutons, optional

1. In a Dutch oven, melt butter over medium-high heat. Add celery, carrots and onion; saute until crisp-tender. Add broccoli and red pepper; stir in broth and pepper. Combine flour and water until smooth; gradually stir into the pan. Bring to a boil. Reduce heat; simmer, uncovered, until thickened and vegetables are tender, 25-30 minutes.

2. Stir in cheeses and beer until cheeses are melted (do not boil). Top with additional shredded cheese, bacon, green onions, sour cream and croutons as desired.

FREEZE OPTION: Before adding toppings, cool soup; transfer to freezer containers. Freeze up to 3 months. To use, partially thaw in refrigerator overnight; heat through in a large saucepan over medium-low heat, stirring occasionally (do not boil). Add toppings if desired.

1 CUP: 316 cal., 23g fat (13g sat. fat), 69mg chol., 1068mg sod., 13g carb. (5g sugars, 2g fiber), 12g pro.

COBB SALAD SUB

COBB SALAD SUB

When we need a quick meal to share, we turn Cobb salad into a jumbo sandwich masterpiece. Sometimes I swap in tortillas for the bread and make wraps instead.
—Kimberly Grusendorf, Medina, OH

- -

TAKES: 15 min. • **MAKES:** 12 servings

- 1 loaf (1 lb.) unsliced Italian bread
- ½ cup balsamic vinaigrette or dressing of your choice
- 5 oz. fresh baby spinach (about 6 cups)
- 1½ lbs. sliced deli ham
- 4 hard-boiled large eggs, finely chopped
- 8 bacon strips, cooked and crumbled
- ½ cup crumbled Gorgonzola cheese
- 1 cup cherry tomatoes, chopped

Cut loaf of bread in half lengthwise; hollow out top and bottom, leaving a ¾-in. shell (discard removed bread or save for another use). Brush vinaigrette over bread halves. Layer spinach, ham, eggs, bacon, cheese and tomatoes on bread bottom. Replace top. Cut loaf in half lengthwise from top to bottom; cut crosswise five times to make 12 total pieces.

1 SLICE: 233 cal., 10g fat (3g sat. fat), 97mg chol., 982mg sod., 17g carb. (3g sugars, 1g fiber), 18g pro.

CHERRY BRIE TOSSED SALAD

Draped in a light vinaigrette and sprinkled with almonds, this pretty salad is a variation of a recipe that's been passed around at school events, church functions and even birthday parties. Everyone wants the recipe. You can also try different cheeses.

—Toni Borden, Wellington, FL

- -

TAKES: 20 min. • **MAKES:** 10 servings

DRESSING
- 1 cup cider vinegar
- ½ cup sugar
- ¼ cup olive oil
- 1 tsp. ground mustard
- 1½ tsp. poppy seeds

SALAD
- 2 Tbsp. butter
- ¾ cup sliced almonds
- 3 Tbsp. sugar
- 8 cups torn romaine
- 1 round (8 oz.) Brie or Camembert cheese, rind removed and cubed
- 1 pkg. (6 oz.) dried cherries

1. In a small bowl, whisk the dressing ingredients; set aside.

2. For salad, in a heavy skillet, melt butter over medium heat. Add almonds; cook and stir until nuts are toasted, about 4 minutes. Sprinkle with sugar; cook and stir until sugar is melted, about 3 minutes. Spread on foil to cool; break apart.

3. In a large salad bowl, combine the romaine, cheese and cherries. Whisk dressing; drizzle over salad. Sprinkle with sugared almonds and toss to coat.

NOTE: Swiss cheese can be used in place of the Brie or Camembert.

1 SERVING: 309 cal., 18g fat (6g sat. fat), 29mg chol., 171mg sod., 32g carb. (27g sugars, 2g fiber), 8g pro.

SPINACH PEAR SALAD WITH CHOCOLATE VINAIGRETTE

SPINACH PEAR SALAD WITH CHOCOLATE VINAIGRETTE

Tangy from balsamic and mellowed with chocolate, the light vinaigrette stays well-blended. It would add an interesting note to berries or watermelon, too.

—*Taste of Home* Test Kitchen

- -

TAKES: 15 min. • **MAKES:** 4 servings

- 1 oz. milk chocolate, chopped
- 3 Tbsp. balsamic vinegar
- 3 Tbsp. canola oil
- 1 tsp. honey
- ¼ tsp. salt
- ⅛ tsp. pepper
- 1 pkg. (6 oz.) fresh baby spinach
- 1 large pear, sliced
- 3 Tbsp. dried cranberries
- 2 Tbsp. sliced almonds, toasted

1. In a microwave, melt chocolate; stir until smooth. Whisk in the vinegar, oil, honey, salt and pepper; set aside.

2. Divide spinach among four salad plates. Top with pear, cranberries and almonds. Drizzle with dressing.

1 SERVING: 215 cal., 14g fat (2g sat. fat), 1mg chol., 185mg sod., 23g carb. (16g sugars, 3g fiber), 3g pro. **DIABETIC EXCHANGES:** 2 fat, 1 starch, 1 vegetable.

TEST KITCHEN TIP

Chocolate can scorch over high heat, so try melting it slowly in the microwave. Remember that chips and chunks may still appear formed and unmelted after heating but will be fluid upon stirring.

TORTILLA SOUP

The presentation of this soup is so pretty, and its zippy flavor is even better!
—Julie Ferron, Wauwatosa, WI

PREP: 30 min. • **COOK:** 50 min.
MAKES: 6 servings

- 1 medium dried ancho pepper, seeded and chopped
- 1 cup water
  Oil for deep-fat frying
- 6 corn tortillas (6 in.), halved and cut into ¼-in. strips
- 1 small onion, sliced
- 4 garlic cloves, peeled
- 1 can (14½ oz.) whole tomatoes, drained
- 6 cups vegetable or chicken broth
- ¼ cup chopped fresh cilantro
- ½ tsp. salt
- ⅛ tsp. cayenne pepper, optional
- 1½ cups shredded Monterey Jack cheese
- 1 large avocado, peeled and diced
- 1 medium lime, sliced and quartered

1. In a small bowl, combine the ancho pepper and water; let stand for 20 minutes or until pepper is softened. Drain and discard water; set pepper aside.

2. In a large saucepan, heat 1 in. of oil to 350°. Add half of the tortilla strips; cook and stir until golden brown. Remove with a slotted spoon to paper towels to drain. Repeat with remaining strips; set aside.

3. Drain saucepan, reserving 2 tsp. of oil. In reserved oil, cook the onion, garlic and ancho pepper over low heat until onion is golden brown, about 7 minutes. Remove from the heat; cool slightly. Transfer to a food processor; add tomatoes. Cover and process until smooth.

4. Return mixture to the pan. Cook, uncovered, over medium heat until mixture has thickened to the consistency of tomato paste, 10 minutes. Add broth; bring to a boil. Reduce heat; cover and simmer for 30 minutes.

5. Add the cilantro, salt and, if desired, cayenne. Divide cheese and avocado among six bowls; top with the soup, tortilla strips and quartered lime slices.

1 CUP: 317 calories, 21g fat (7g saturated fat), 25mg cholesterol, 1154mg sodium, 23g carbohydrate (4g sugars, 6g fiber), 11g protein.

FOCACCIA SANDWICHES

Slices of this pretty sandwich make any casual get-together a bit more special. Add or change ingredients to your taste.
—Peggy Woodward, Senior Food Editor

TAKES: 15 min. • **MAKES:** 2 dozen

- ⅓ cup mayonnaise
- 1 can (4¼ oz.) chopped ripe olives, drained
- 1 focaccia bread (about 12 oz.), halved lengthwise
- 4 romaine leaves
- ¼ lb. shaved deli ham
- 1 medium sweet red pepper, thinly sliced into rings
- ¼ lb. shaved deli turkey
- 1 large tomato, thinly sliced
- ¼ lb. thinly sliced hard salami
- 1 jar (7 oz.) roasted sweet red peppers, drained
- 4 to 6 slices provolone cheese

In a small bowl, combine mayonnaise and olives; spread over the bottom half of bread. Layer with remaining ingredients; replace the bread top. Cut into 24 wedges; secure with toothpicks.

1 PIECE: 113 cal., 6g fat (2g sat. fat), 13mg chol., 405mg sod., 9g carb. (1g sugars, 1g fiber), 5g pro.

TORTILLA SOUP

FLAVORFUL CHICKEN
FAJITAS, PAGE 70

Entrees

It was nearly impossible to get our Test Kitchen staff to agree on which *Taste of Home* main courses they prepare most—there are just too many! These mouthwatering recipes landed at the top of the list as the entrees that our cooks serve to their own families. Try one tonight for surefire success at your table.

ROASTED CHICKEN
WITH ROSEMARY

ROASTED CHICKEN WITH ROSEMARY

Herbs, garlic and butter give this hearty meal-in-one a classic flavor everyone raves about. It's a lot like pot roast, only it uses chicken instead of beef.
—Isabel Zienkosky, Salt Lake City, UT

PREP: 20 min. • **BAKE:** 2 hours + standing
MAKES: 9 servings

- ½ cup butter, cubed
- 4 Tbsp. minced fresh rosemary or 2 Tbsp. dried rosemary, crushed
- 2 Tbsp. minced fresh parsley
- 1 tsp. salt
- ½ tsp. pepper
- 3 garlic cloves, minced
- 1 whole roasting chicken (5 to 6 lbs.)
- 6 small red potatoes, halved
- 6 medium carrots, halved lengthwise and cut into 2-in. pieces
- 2 medium onions, quartered

1. In a small saucepan, melt butter; stir in the seasonings and garlic. Place chicken breast side up on a rack in a shallow roasting pan; tie drumsticks together with kitchen string. Spoon half the butter mixture over the chicken. Place the potatoes, carrots and onions around chicken. Drizzle remaining butter mixture over vegetables.
2. Bake at 350° for 1½ hours. Baste with cooking juices; bake 30-60 minutes longer, basting occasionally, until a thermometer inserted in thickest part of thigh reads 170°-175°. (Cover loosely with foil if the chicken browns too quickly.)
3. Let stand for 10-15 minutes, tented with foil if necessary, before carving. Serve with the vegetables.
1 SERVING: 449 cal., 28g fat (11g sat. fat), 126mg chol., 479mg sod., 16g carb. (5g sugars, 3g fiber), 33g pro.

THREE-CHEESE SOUFFLES

No matter when I've made these souffles, they have always been a success. Although I've never seen the centers start to fall, it's best to serve them hot from the oven.
—Jean Ference, Sherwood Park, AB

PREP: 40 min. + cooling • **BAKE:** 40 min.
MAKES: 8 servings

- ⅓ cup butter, cubed
- ⅓ cup all-purpose flour

THREE-CHEESE SOUFFLES

- 2 cups whole milk
- 1 tsp. Dijon mustard
- ¼ tsp. salt
  Dash hot pepper sauce
- 1½ cups shredded Swiss cheese
- 1 cup shredded cheddar cheese
- ¼ cup shredded Parmesan cheese
- 6 large eggs
- ½ tsp. cream of tartar

1. In a small saucepan, melt butter over medium heat. Stir in flour until smooth; cook 1 minute. Gradually whisk in milk, mustard, salt and pepper sauce. Bring to a boil, stirring constantly; cook and stir 1-2 minutes or until thickened. Reduce heat to medium-low; stir in the cheeses until melted. Transfer to a large bowl.
2. Separate eggs. Place the egg whites in a medium bowl; let stand at room temperature 30 minutes. Meanwhile, in a small bowl, beat egg yolks until thick and lemon-colored, about 4 minutes. Stir in ⅓ cup hot cheese mixture; return all to the remaining cheese mixture, stirring constantly. Cool completely.
3. Preheat oven to 325°. Place eight ungreased 8-oz. ramekins in a baking pan.
4. With clean beaters, beat egg whites with cream of tartar on high speed until stiff but not dry. With a rubber spatula, gently stir a fourth of the egg whites into cheese mixture. Fold in remaining whites.
5. Transfer to prepared ramekins. Add 1 in. of hot water to baking pan. Bake 40-45 minutes or until tops are golden brown. Serve immediately.
FREEZE OPTION: Securely wrap unbaked souffles with foil and freeze. To use, preheat oven to 325°. Remove foil and place frozen souffles in a baking pan; add 1 in. warm water to larger pan. Bake 60-65 minutes or until heated through and tops are golden brown.
1 SOUFFLE: 317 cal., 24g fat (14g sat. fat), 223mg chol., 424mg sod., 9g carb. (4g sugars, 0 fiber), 17g pro.

GARLIC GRILLED STEAKS

For a mouthwatering change at your next barbecue, take steak to new flavor heights! Simply baste your choice of cuts with this garlicky blend that requires only a few minutes to fix.
—*Taste of Home* Test Kitchen

- -

TAKES: 15 min. • **MAKES:** 4 servings

- 10   garlic cloves
- 1½   tsp. salt
- ½   tsp. pepper
- 2   Tbsp. olive oil
- 1   Tbsp. lemon juice
- 2   tsp. Worcestershire sauce
- 4   boneless beef strip steaks or ribeye steaks (1 in. thick and 8 oz. each)

1. With a mortar and pestle, crush garlic cloves with salt and pepper. Stir in oil, lemon juice and Worcestershire sauce.
2. Grill steaks, covered, over medium heat 5-7 minutes on each side or until meat reaches desired doneness (for medium-rare, a thermometer should read 135°; medium, 140°; medium-well, 145°). Brush generously with garlic mixture during the last four minutes of cooking.
NOTE: Strip steak may be labeled as club, New York strip, Kansas City or top loin steak.
1 STEAK: 373 cal., 17g fat (5g sat. fat), 100mg chol., 1013mg sod., 3g carb. (0 sugars, 0 fiber), 48g pro.

STIR-FRIED
SCALLOPS

STIR-FRIED SCALLOPS

Scallops add interest to this mild tomato-based stovetop supper that's perfect for small households. It's nearly impossible to believe this dinner comes together in just a few moments.
—Stephany Gocobachi, San Rafael, CA

- -

TAKES: 15 min. • **MAKES:** 2 servings

- 1   small onion, chopped
- 3   garlic cloves, minced
- 1   Tbsp. olive oil
- ¾   lb. sea scallops, halved
- 2   medium plum tomatoes, chopped
- 2   Tbsp. lemon juice
- ⅛   tsp. pepper
     Hot cooked pasta or rice, optional

1. In a nonstick skillet or wok, stir-fry onion and garlic in hot oil until tender. Add the scallops; stir-fry until scallops turn opaque. Add tomatoes; cook and stir until heated through, 1-2 minutes longer.
2. Stir in lemon juice and pepper. Serve over pasta or rice if desired.
1 CUP: 213 cal., 8g fat (1g sat. fat), 41mg chol., 672mg sod., 14g carb. (4g sugars, 2g fiber), 22g pro.

TATER-TOPPED CASSEROLE

I often make this all-in-one dish ahead of time and reheat it for potlucks.
—Rosa Dietzler, Santa Rosa, CA

- -

PREP: 15 min. • **BAKE:** 1 hour
MAKES: 8 servings

- 1½   lbs. ground beef
- 1   pkg. (16 oz.) frozen vegetables, thawed
- 1   can (2.8 oz.) french-fried onions
- ¼   cup butter
- 1   can (10¾ oz.) condensed cream of celery soup, undiluted
- 1   can (10¾ oz.) condensed cream of chicken soup, undiluted
- ½   cup whole milk
- 1   pkg. (16 oz.) frozen Tater Tots, thawed

1. In a large skillet, cook beef over medium heat until no longer pink; drain. In a greased 13x9-in. baking dish, layer the beef, vegetables and onions. Dot with butter.
2. In a bowl, combine soups and milk; spread over the vegetables. Top with Tater Tots. Bake, uncovered, at 350° for 1 hour or until golden brown.
1 SERVING: 482 cal., 31g fat (12g sat. fat), 78mg chol., 1006mg sod., 32g carb. (3g sugars, 4g fiber), 22g pro.

CALGARY STAMPEDE RIBS

"More, please!" is what I hear when I serve these finger-licking ribs. The first time my husband and I tried them, we pronounced them the best ever. After just one bite, you won't want to prepare your ribs any other way again.
—Marian Misik, Sherwood Park, AB

- -

PREP: 2¼ hours + marinating
GRILL: 15 min. • **MAKES:** 8 servings

- 4 lbs. pork baby back ribs, cut into serving-size pieces
- 3 garlic cloves, minced
- 1 Tbsp. sugar
- 2 tsp. salt
- 1 Tbsp. paprika
- 2 tsp. ground cumin
- 2 tsp. chili powder
- 2 tsp. pepper

BARBECUE SAUCE
- 2 Tbsp. butter
- 1 small onion, finely chopped
- 1 cup ketchup
- ¼ cup packed brown sugar
- 3 Tbsp. lemon juice
- 3 Tbsp. Worcestershire sauce
- 2 Tbsp. cider vinegar
- 1½ tsp. ground mustard
- 1 tsp. celery seed
- ⅛ tsp. cayenne pepper

1. Preheat oven to 325°. Rub ribs with garlic; place in a roasting pan. Bake, covered, until tender, about 2 hours.

2. Mix the sugar, salt and spices; sprinkle over ribs. Remove from pan; cool slightly. Refrigerate, covered, 8 hours or overnight.

3. In a small saucepan, heat butter over medium heat; saute onion until tender. Stir in the remaining ingredients; bring to a boil. Reduce the heat; cook, uncovered, until thickened, about 10 minutes, stirring frequently.

4. Brush ribs with some of the sauce. Grill, covered, over medium heat until heated through, 12-15 minutes, turning and brushing occasionally with additional sauce. Serve with remaining sauce.

1 SERVING: 990 cal., 68g fat (26g sat. fat), 260mg chol., 2307mg sod., 42g carb. (25g sugars, 3g fiber), 53g pro.

CALGARY STAMPEDE RIBS

SUNDAY CHOPS & STUFFING

My family likes it when I make these chops for Sunday dinner. The recipe lets us spend more time having fun together and less time working in the kitchen.
—Georgiann Franklin, Canfield, OH

- -

PREP: 30 min. • **BAKE:** 25 min.
MAKES: 6 servings

- 2 cups water
- 2 celery ribs, chopped (about 1 cup)
- 7 Tbsp. butter, divided
- ¼ cup dried minced onion
- 6 cups seasoned stuffing cubes
- 1 Tbsp. canola oil
- 6 bone-in pork loin chops (7 oz. each)
- ¼ tsp. salt
- ¼ tsp. pepper
- 2 medium tart apples, sliced
- ¼ cup packed brown sugar
- ⅛ tsp. pumpkin pie spice

1. Preheat oven to 350°. In a large saucepan, combine water, celery, 6 Tbsp. butter and onion. Bring to a boil. Remove from heat; stir in stuffing cubes. Spoon into a greased 13x9-in. baking dish.

2. In a large skillet, heat oil over medium heat. Brown pork chops on both sides. Arrange over stuffing. Sprinkle with salt and pepper. In a small bowl, toss apples with brown sugar and pie spice; place over pork chops. Dot with remaining butter.

3. Bake, uncovered, 25-30 minutes or until a thermometer inserted in pork reads 145°. Let stand 5 minutes before serving.

1 SERVING: 600 cal., 26g fat (12g sat. fat), 122mg chol., 1018mg sod., 56g carb. (19g sugars, 4g fiber), 36g pro.

FOUR-CHEESE SPINACH LASAGNA

FOUR-CHEESE SPINACH LASAGNA

This rich cheesy lasagna has become one of my specialties. It's packed with fresh-tasting vegetables, including broccoli, spinach and red pepper. I'm never afraid to serve the colorful casserole to guests, since it is always a huge success.
—Kimberly Kneisly, Englewood, OH

PREP: 50 min. • **BAKE:** 50 min. + standing
MAKES: 12 servings

  2 cups chopped fresh broccoli
1½ cups julienned carrots
  1 cup sliced green onions
  ½ cup chopped sweet red pepper
  3 garlic cloves, minced
  2 tsp. vegetable oil
  ½ cup all-purpose flour
  3 cups whole milk
  ½ cup grated Parmesan cheese, divided
  ½ tsp. salt
  ¼ tsp. pepper
  1 pkg. (10 oz.) frozen chopped spinach, thawed and squeezed dry
1½ cups 4% cottage cheese
  1 cup shredded part-skim mozzarella cheese
  ½ cup shredded Swiss cheese
 12 lasagna noodles, cooked and drained

1. In a large skillet, saute vegetables and garlic in oil until crisp-tender. Remove from the heat; set aside.
2. In a small heavy saucepan, whisk flour and milk until smooth. Bring to a boil; cook and stir for 2 minutes. Reduce heat; stir in ¼ cup Parmesan cheese, salt and pepper. Cook 1 minute longer or until cheese is melted. Remove from the heat; stir in spinach. Set 1 cup aside.
3. In a large bowl, combine the cottage cheese, mozzarella and Swiss cheese. Spread ½ cup spinach mixture in a greased 13x9-in. baking dish. Layer with four noodles, half the cheese mixture, half the vegetables and ¾ cup spinach mixture. Repeat layers. Top with remaining noodles, reserved spinach mixture and remaining Parmesan cheese.
4. Cover and bake at 375° for 35 minutes. Uncover; bake 15 minutes longer or until bubbly. Let stand 15 minutes before cutting.
1 PIECE: 277 cal., 9g fat (5g sat. fat), 22mg chol., 415mg sod., 33g carb. (8g sugars, 3g fiber), 16g pro. **DIABETIC EXCHANGES:** 2 starch, 2 medium-fat meat.

SLOW-COOKED HERBED TURKEY

I prepare this recipe when herbs are plentiful in my garden. The turkey stays moist in the slow cooker and bursts with herb flavors. Everyone in our Bible study potluck group wanted the recipe!
—Sue Jurack, Mequon, WI

PREP: 15 min. + marinating
COOK: 4 hours + standing
MAKES: 16 servings

  2 cans (14½ oz. each) chicken broth
  1 cup lemon juice
  ½ cup packed brown sugar
  ½ cup minced fresh sage
  ½ cup minced fresh thyme
  ½ cup lime juice
  ½ cup cider vinegar
  ½ cup olive oil
  2 envelopes onion soup mix
  ¼ cup Dijon mustard
  2 Tbsp. minced fresh marjoram
  3 tsp. paprika
  2 tsp. garlic powder
  2 tsp. pepper
  1 tsp. salt
  2 boneless skinless turkey breast halves (3 lbs. each)

1. Combine the first 15 ingredients in a blender; cover and process until blended. Place turkey breasts in a gallon-size resealable plastic bag; add half of marinade. Seal bag and turn to coat; seal and refrigerate overnight. Pour remaining marinade into a bowl; cover and refrigerate.
2. Drain and discard marinade from turkey. Transfer turkey breasts to a 5-qt. slow cooker. Add reserved marinade; cover and cook on high for 4-5 hours or until a thermometer reads 170°. Let stand for 10 minutes before slicing.
5 OZ. COOKED TURKEY: 232 cal., 5g fat (1g sat. fat), 97mg chol., 369mg sod., 4g carb. (3g sugars, 0 fiber), 40g pro. **DIABETIC EXCHANGES:** 5 lean meat, ½ fat.

READER RAVE

"I made this for Thanksgiving; it was a big hit. I loved it because I made it the day before in the slow cooker. Great recipe, and I will be making it again."
—RESA1979, TASTEOFHOME.COM

SLOW-COOKED
HERBED TURKEY

SLICED HAM WITH ROASTED VEGETABLES

To prepare this colorful, zesty oven meal, I shop in my backyard for the fresh garden vegetables that spark the ham's hearty flavor. It's my family's favorite main dish.
—Margaret Pache, Mesa, AZ

- -

PREP: 10 min. • **BAKE:** 35 min.
MAKES: 6 servings

- 6 medium potatoes, peeled and cubed
- 5 medium carrots, sliced
- 1 medium turnip, peeled and cubed
- 1 large onion, cut into thin wedges
- 6 slices (4 to 6 oz. each) fully cooked ham, halved
- ¼ cup thawed orange juice concentrate
- 2 Tbsp. brown sugar
- 1 tsp. prepared horseradish
- 1 tsp. grated orange zest
  Coarsely ground pepper

1. Grease two 15x10x1-in. baking pans with cooking spray. Add potatoes, carrots, turnip and onion; generously coat with cooking spray. Bake, uncovered, at 425° until tender, 25-30 minutes.
2. Arrange ham slices over the vegetables. In a bowl, combine concentrate, brown sugar, horseradish and orange zest. Spoon over ham and vegetables. Bake until the ham is heated through, 10 minutes longer. Sprinkle with pepper.
1 SERVING: 375 cal., 5g fat (1g sat. fat), 71mg chol., 1179mg sod., 55g carb. (15g sugars, 7g fiber), 31g pro.

HARVESTTIME CHICKEN WITH COUSCOUS

Even on busy days, I can start this chicken in a slow cooker and still get to work on time. When I come home, I add a spinach salad and crescent rolls.
—Heidi Rudolph, Oregon, IL

- -

PREP: 30 min. • **COOK:** 3 hours
MAKES: 6 servings

- 2 medium sweet potatoes (about 1¼ lbs.), peeled and cut into ½-in. pieces
- 1 medium sweet red pepper, coarsely chopped
- 1½ lbs. boneless skinless chicken breasts
- 1 can (14½ oz.) stewed tomatoes, undrained
- ½ cup peach or mango salsa
- ¼ cup golden raisins
- ½ tsp. salt
- ¼ tsp. ground cumin
- ¼ tsp. ground cinnamon
- ¼ tsp. pepper

COUSCOUS
- 1 cup water
- ½ tsp. salt
- 1 cup uncooked whole wheat couscous

1. In a 4-qt. slow cooker, layer sweet potatoes, red pepper and chicken breasts. In a small bowl, mix tomatoes, salsa, raisins and seasonings; pour over chicken. Cook, covered, on low 3-4 hours or until sweet potatoes and chicken are tender.
2. About 10 minutes before serving, prepare couscous. In a small saucepan, bring water and salt to a boil. Stir in couscous. Remove from heat; let stand, covered, 5 minutes or until water is absorbed. Fluff with a fork.
3. Remove chicken from slow cooker; coarsely shred with two forks. Return chicken to slow cooker, stirring gently to combine. Serve with couscous.
FREEZE OPTION: Place cooled chicken mixture in freezer containers. To use, partially thaw in refrigerator overnight. Microwave, covered, on high in a microwave-safe dish until heated through, stirring gently; add a little broth or water if necessary.
1⅓ CUPS CHICKEN MIXTURE WITH ½ CUP COUSCOUS: 351 cal., 3g fat (1g sat. fat), 63mg chol., 699mg sod., 52g carb. (15g sugars, 7g fiber), 30g pro.

HARVESTTIME CHICKEN WITH COUSCOUS

CHICAGO-STYLE DEEP-DISH PIZZA

CHICAGO-STYLE DEEP-DISH PIZZA

My husband and I tried to duplicate the pizza from a popular Chicago restaurant, and I think our recipe turned out even better. We found that the secret is baking it in a cast-iron skillet.

—Lynn Hamilton, Naperville, IL

PREP: 20 min. + rising • **BAKE:** 40 min.
MAKES: 2 pizzas (8 slices each)

- 3½ cups all-purpose flour
- ¼ cup cornmeal
- 1 pkg. (¼ oz.) quick-rise yeast
- 1½ tsp. sugar
- ½ tsp. salt
- 1 cup water
- ⅓ cup olive oil

TOPPINGS

- 6 cups shredded part-skim mozzarella cheese, divided
- 1 can (28 oz.) diced tomatoes, well drained
- 1 can (8 oz.) tomato sauce
- 1 can (6 oz.) tomato paste
- ½ tsp. salt
- ¼ tsp. each garlic powder, dried oregano, dried basil and pepper
- 1 lb. bulk Italian sausage, cooked and crumbled
- 48 slices pepperoni
- ½ lb. sliced fresh mushrooms
- ¼ cup grated Parmesan cheese

1. In a large bowl, combine 1½ cups flour, cornmeal, yeast, sugar and salt. In a saucepan, heat water and oil to 120°-130°. Add to dry ingredients; beat just until moistened. Add remaining flour to form a stiff dough.

2. Turn onto a floured surface; knead until smooth and elastic, 6-8 minutes. Place in a greased bowl, turning once to grease top. Cover and let rise in warm place until doubled, about 30 minutes.

3. Punch dough down; divide in half. Roll each portion into an 11-in. circle. Press dough onto the bottom and up the sides of two greased 10-in. ovenproof skillets. Sprinkle each with 2 cups mozzarella cheese.

4. In a large bowl, combine the tomatoes, tomato sauce, tomato paste and seasonings. Spoon 1½ cups over each pizza. Layer each with half of the sausage, pepperoni and mushrooms; 1 cup mozzarella; and 2 Tbsp. Parmesan cheese.

5. Cover and bake at 450° for 35 minutes. Uncover; bake 5 minutes longer or until lightly browned.

NOTE: Two 9-in. springform pans may be used in place of the skillet. Place pans on baking sheets. Run knife around edge of pan to loosen crust before removing sides.

1 SLICE: 384 cal., 21g fat (9g sat. fat), 50mg chol., 837mg sod., 32g carb. (6g sugars, 2g fiber), 17g pro.

SPRING-THYME CHICKEN STEW

During a long winter (and spring), my husband and I were in need of something warm, comforting and bright. This chicken was the perfect thing. I love it because its incredible aroma reminds me of my mom's homemade chicken soup.

—Amy Chase, Vanderhoof, BC

PREP: 15 min. • **COOK:** 7 hours
MAKES: 4 servings

- 1 lb. small red potatoes, halved
- 1 large onion, finely chopped
- ¾ cup shredded carrots
- 3 Tbsp. all-purpose flour
- 6 garlic cloves, minced
- 2 tsp. grated lemon peel
- 2 tsp. dried thyme
- ½ tsp. salt
- ¼ tsp. pepper
- 1½ lbs. boneless skinless chicken thighs, halved
- 2 cups reduced-sodium chicken broth
- 2 bay leaves
- 2 Tbsp. minced fresh parsley

1. Place potatoes, onion and carrots in a 3-qt. slow cooker. Sprinkle with flour, garlic, lemon peel, thyme, salt and pepper; toss to coat. Place chicken over top. Add broth and bay leaves.

2. Cook, covered, on low 7-9 hours or until chicken and vegetables are tender. Remove bay leaves. Sprinkle servings with parsley.

1 SERVING: 395 cal., 13g fat (3g sat. fat), 113mg chol., 707mg sod., 32g carb. (5g sugars, 4g fiber), 37g pro. **DIABETIC EXCHANGES:** 5 lean meat, 2 vegetable, 1½ starch.

GRILLED
GARDEN
PIZZA

GRILLED GARDEN PIZZA

Dazzle your family and friends with pizzas fresh off the grill. We top them with Asiago, Parmesan, veggies and fresh basil. Pile on the toppings you love.

—Teri Rasey, Cadillac, MI

- -

TAKES: 30 min. • **MAKES:** 6 servings

2 plum tomatoes, thinly sliced
½ tsp. sea salt or kosher salt
1 loaf (1 lb.) frozen pizza
    dough, thawed
2 Tbsp. olive oil, divided
½ cup shredded Parmesan
    or Asiago cheese
½ cup fresh or frozen corn, thawed
¼ cup thinly sliced red onion
8 oz. fresh mozzarella cheese, sliced
½ cup thinly sliced fresh spinach
3 Tbsp. chopped fresh basil

1. Sprinkle tomatoes with salt; set aside. On a lightly floured surface, divide dough in half. Roll or press each to ¼-in. thickness; place each on a greased sheet of foil (about 10 in. square). Brush tops with 1 Tbsp. oil.
2. Carefully invert crusts onto grill rack, removing foil. Brush tops with remaining oil. Grill, covered, over medium heat 2-3 minutes or until bottom is golden brown. Remove from grill; reduce grill temperature to low.
3. Top grilled sides of crusts with Parmesan or Asiago cheese, tomatoes, corn, onion and mozzarella cheese. Grill, covered, on low heat 4-6 minutes or until cheese is melted. Sprinkle with spinach and basil.
1 PIECE: 375 cal., 16g fat (7g sat. fat), 35mg chol., 680mg sod., 40g carb. (4g sugars, 1g fiber), 15g pro.

TEST KITCHEN TIP
Fresh mozzarella has about the same calories and fat as part-skim. That said, they are both lighter than a lot of other cheeses such as cheddar, Muenster and provolone.

TACO-FILLED PASTA SHELLS

TACO-FILLED PASTA SHELLS

I've been stuffing pasta shells with different fillings for years, but my family enjoys this version with taco-seasoned meat the most. I like to freeze the shells because you can take out only the number you need for a single-serving lunch or family dinner. Just add zippy taco sauce and bake.

—Marge Hodel, Roanoke, IL

- -

PREP: 20 min. + chilling • **BAKE:** 45 min.
MAKES: 2 casseroles (6 servings each)

2 lbs. ground beef
2 envelopes taco seasoning
1½ cups water
1 pkg. (8 oz.) cream cheese, cubed
24 uncooked jumbo pasta shells
¼ cup butter, melted
ADDITIONAL INGREDIENTS
      (FOR EACH CASSEROLE)
1 cup salsa
1 cup taco sauce
1 cup shredded cheddar cheese
1 cup shredded Monterey Jack cheese
1½ cups crushed tortilla chips
1 cup sour cream
3 green onions, chopped

1. In a Dutch oven, cook beef over medium heat until no longer pink; drain. Stir in taco seasoning and water. Bring to a boil. Reduce heat; simmer, uncovered, for 5 minutes. Stir in cream cheese until melted. Transfer to a bowl; cool. Chill for 1 hour.
2. Cook pasta according to the package directions; drain. Gently toss with butter. Fill each shell with about 3 Tbsp. of meat mixture. Place 12 shells in a freezer container. Cover and freeze for up to 3 months.
3. To prepare remaining shells, spoon salsa into a greased 9-in. square baking dish. Top with stuffed shells and taco sauce. Cover and bake at 350° for 30 minutes. Uncover; sprinkle with cheeses and chips. Bake for 15 minutes longer or until heated through. Serve with sour cream and onions.
TO USE FROZEN SHELLS: Thaw shells in the refrigerator for 24 hours (shells will be partially frozen). Spoon salsa into a greased 9-in. square baking dish; top with shells and taco sauce. Cover and bake at 350° for 40 minutes. Uncover; continue as above.
2 SHELLS: 492 cal., 31g fat (16g sat. fat), 98mg chol., 982mg sod., 29g carb. (4g sugars, 1g fiber), 23g pro.

BRUSCHETTA CHICKEN

We enjoy serving this tasty chicken to both family and to company. It just might become your new favorite way to use up summer tomatoes and basil.

—Carolin Cattoi-Demkiw, Lethbridge, AB

PREP: 10 min. • **BAKE:** 30 min.
MAKES: 4 servings

- ½ cup all-purpose flour
- ½ cup egg substitute
- 4 boneless skinless chicken breast halves (4 oz. each)
- ¼ cup grated Parmesan cheese
- ¼ cup dry bread crumbs
- 1 Tbsp. butter, melted
- 2 large tomatoes, seeded and chopped
- 3 Tbsp. minced fresh basil
- 1 Tbsp. olive oil
- 2 garlic cloves, minced
- ½ tsp. salt
- ¼ tsp. pepper

1. Preheat oven to 375°. Place flour and egg substitute in separate shallow bowls. Dip chicken in flour, then in egg substitute; place in a greased 13x9-in. baking dish. In a small bowl, mix cheese, bread crumbs and butter; sprinkle over chicken.

2. Loosely cover baking dish with foil. Bake 20 minutes. Uncover; bake 5-10 minutes longer or until a thermometer reads 165°.

3. Meanwhile, in a small bowl, toss tomatoes with the remaining ingredients. Spoon over chicken; bake 3-5 minutes or until tomato mixture is heated through.

1 SERVING: 316 cal., 11g fat (4g sat. fat), 75mg chol., 563mg sod., 22g carb. (4g sugars, 2g fiber), 31g pro. **DIABETIC EXCHANGES:** 3 lean meat, 1½ fat, 1 starch, 1 vegetable.

SWEET & TANGY SALMON
WITH GREEN BEANS

SWEET & TANGY SALMON WITH GREEN BEANS

I'm always up for new ways to cook salmon. In this dish, a sweet sauce gives the fish and green beans some down-home barbecue tang. Even our kids love it.

—Aliesha Caldwell, Robersonville, NC

PREP: 20 min. • **BAKE:** 15 min.
MAKES: 4 servings

- 4 salmon fillets (6 oz. each)
- 1 Tbsp. butter
- 2 Tbsp. brown sugar
- 2 Tbsp. reduced-sodium soy sauce
- 2 Tbsp. Dijon mustard
- 1 Tbsp. olive oil
- ½ tsp. pepper
- ⅛ tsp. salt
- 1 lb. fresh green beans, trimmed

1. Preheat oven to 425°. Place fillets in a 15x10x1-in. baking pan coated with cooking spray. In a small skillet, melt butter; stir in brown sugar, soy sauce, mustard, oil, pepper and salt. Brush half of the mixture over salmon.

2. Place green beans in a large bowl; drizzle with remaining brown sugar mixture and toss to coat. Arrange green beans around fillets. Roast until fish just begins to flake easily with a fork and green beans are crisp-tender, 14-16 minutes.

1 FILLET WITH ¾ CUP GREEN BEANS: 394 cal., 22g fat (5g sat. fat), 93mg chol., 661mg sod., 17g carb. (10g sugars, 4g fiber), 31g pro. **DIABETIC EXCHANGES:** 5 lean meat, 1½ fat, 1 vegetable, ½ starch.

TEST KITCHEN TIP

It's wise to buy salmon fillets that are roughly the same thickness so they cook evenly. If you're craving Asian flavors, add ½ tsp. minced fresh ginger to the sauce and use sesame oil instead of olive oil. Either way, make cleanup a breeze by lining a sheet pan with foil or using a disposable pan.

CARIBBEAN CHICKEN

You'd be hard-pressed to find a marinade that's this flavorful from any store! Add or subtract the jalapenos to suit your gang's taste, and you'll be grilling a new family favorite before you know it.
—Rusty Collins, Orlando, FL

- -

PREP: 15 min. + marinating • **GRILL:** 10 min.
MAKES: 6 servings

- ½   cup lemon juice
- ⅓   cup honey
- 3   Tbsp. canola oil
- 6   green onions, sliced
- 3   jalapeno peppers, seeded and chopped
- 3   tsp. dried thyme
- ¾   tsp. salt
- ¼   tsp. ground allspice
- ¼   tsp. ground nutmeg
- 6   boneless skinless chicken breast halves (4 oz. each)

1. In a blender, combine the first nine ingredients; cover and process until smooth. Pour ½ cup into a small bowl for basting; cover and refrigerate. Pour remaining marinade into a large resealable plastic bag; add chicken. Seal bag and turn to coat; refrigerate for up to 6 hours.
2. Drain chicken, discarding marinade. On a greased grill rack, grill chicken, covered, over medium heat or broil 4 in. from the heat for 4-6 minutes on each side or until a thermometer reads 165°, basting frequently with the reserved marinade.
NOTE: Wear disposable gloves when cutting hot peppers; the oils can burn skin. Avoid touching your face.
1 CHICKEN BREAST HALF: 186 cal., 6g fat (1g sat. fat), 63mg chol., 204mg sod., 9g carb. (8g sugars, 0 fiber), 23g pro. **DIABETIC EXCHANGES:** 3 lean meat, ½ starch, ½ fat.

SMOKED MOZZARELLA CHICKEN WITH PASTA

Take an ordinary chicken breast into "wow territory" with just a few extra ingredients. Use prosciutto instead of ham to make the dish extra smoky.
—Naylet LaRochelle, Miami, FL

- -

TAKES: 30 min. • **MAKES:** 4 servings

- 8   oz. uncooked angel hair pasta or thin spaghetti
- 4   boneless skinless chicken breast halves (6 oz. each)
- ½   tsp. salt
- ¼   tsp. pepper
- ⅔   cup seasoned bread crumbs
- 2   Tbsp. olive oil
- 4   thin slices smoked deli ham
- 4   slices smoked mozzarella cheese
- ½   tsp. dried sage leaves
- ½   cup prepared pesto
      Grated Parmesan cheese, optional

1. Cook pasta according to package directions. Drain; transfer to a large bowl.
2. Meanwhile, pound chicken breasts with a meat mallet to ½-in. thickness; sprinkle with salt and pepper. Place bread crumbs in a shallow bowl. Dip chicken in bread crumbs to coat both sides; shake off excess.
3. In a large skillet, heat oil over medium-high heat. Add chicken; cook 4 minutes. Turn; cook 2 minutes longer. Top with ham and mozzarella cheese; sprinkle with sage. Cook 1-2 minutes longer or until a thermometer inserted in chicken reads 165°. Remove from the heat.
4. Add pesto to pasta and toss to coat. Serve chicken with pasta. If desired, sprinkle with Parmesan cheese.
1 CHICKEN BREAST HALF WITH ¾ CUP PASTA: 694 cal., 28g fat (7g sat. fat), 122mg chol., 1184mg sod., 53g carb. (4g sugars, 3g fiber), 53g pro.

CARIBBEAN CHICKEN

LEMON-BATTER FISH

Here's a delicious classic! You'll love what the light and crispy batter does for your fresh catch.
—Jackie Hannahs, Cedar Springs, MI

- -

TAKES: 25 min. • **MAKES:** 6 servings

- 1½ cups all-purpose flour, divided
- 1 tsp. baking powder
- ¾ tsp. salt
- ½ tsp. sugar
- 1 large egg, lightly beaten
- ⅔ cup water
- ⅔ cup lemon juice, divided
- 2 lbs. perch or walleye fillets, cut into serving-size pieces
  Oil for frying
  Lemon wedges, optional

1. Combine 1 cup flour, baking powder, salt and sugar. In another bowl, combine egg, water and ⅓ cup lemon juice; stir into dry ingredients until smooth.
2. Place remaining lemon juice and remaining flour in shallow bowls. Dip fillets in lemon juice, then flour, then coat with egg mixture.
3. In a large skillet, heat 1 in. oil over medium-high heat. Fry fillets until golden brown and fish flakes easily with a fork, 2-3 minutes each side. Drain on paper towels. If desired, serve with lemon wedges.
5 OZ. COOKED FISH: 384 cal., 17g fat (2g sat.fat), 167mg chol., 481mg sod., 22g carb. (1g sugars, 1g fiber), 33g pro.
LIME-BATTER FISH: Substitute lime juice for the lemon juice.

FLAVORFUL CHICKEN FAJITAS

FLAVORFUL CHICKEN FAJITAS

This chicken fajita recipe is definitely on my weeknight dinner rotation. The marinated chicken in these wraps is as mouthwatering as it gets. The fajitas go together in a snap and always get raves!
—Julie Sterchi, Campbellsville, KY

- -

PREP: 20 min. + marinating • **COOK:** 10 min.
MAKES: 6 servings

- 4 Tbsp. canola oil, divided
- 2 Tbsp. lemon juice
- 1½ tsp. seasoned salt
- 1½ tsp. dried oregano
- 1½ tsp. ground cumin
- 1 tsp. garlic powder
- ½ tsp. chili powder
- ½ tsp. paprika
- ½ tsp. crushed red pepper flakes, optional
- 1½ lbs. boneless skinless chicken breast, cut into thin strips
- ½ medium sweet red pepper, julienned
- ½ medium green pepper, julienned
- 4 green onions, thinly sliced
- ½ cup chopped onion
- 6 flour tortillas (8 in.), warmed
  Shredded cheddar cheese, taco sauce, salsa, guacamole and sour cream, optional

1. In a large bowl, combine 2 Tbsp. oil, lemon juice and seasonings; add the chicken. Turn to coat; cover. Refrigerate for 1-4 hours.
2. In a large skillet, saute peppers and onions in remaining oil until crisp-tender. Remove and keep warm.
3. Drain chicken, discarding marinade. In the same skillet, cook chicken over medium-high heat for 5-6 minutes or until no longer pink. Return pepper mixture to pan; heat through.
4. Spoon filling down the center of tortillas; fold in half. Serve with toppings as desired.
1 FAJITA: 369 cal., 15g fat (2g sat. fat), 63mg chol., 689mg sod., 30g carb. (2g sugars, 1g fiber), 28g pro. **DIABETIC EXCHANGES:** 3 lean meat, 2 starch, 2 fat

LEMON-BATTER FISH

ROSEMARY ROOT
VEGETABLES,
PAGE 78

Side Dishes

Give your meals lip-smacking flair when
you round out menus with any of these
19 veggies and breads. Not only are they all
Test Kitchen-approved, but these are the sides
our staffers rely on to liven up their own dinners.

PESTO-CORN PEPPERS

We grill almost daily and enjoy using fresh produce from our garden. These pepper halves filled with a basil-seasoned corn mixture are my husband's favorite.
—Rachael Marrier, Star Prairie, WI

TAKES: 30 min. • **MAKES:** 8 servings

½ cup plus 2 tsp. olive oil, divided
¾ cup grated Parmesan cheese
2 cups packed basil leaves
2 Tbsp. sunflower kernels or walnuts
4 garlic cloves
½ cup finely chopped sweet red pepper
4 cups fresh or frozen corn, thawed
4 medium sweet red, yellow or green peppers
¼ cup shredded Parmesan cheese, optional

1. For pesto, combine ½ cup oil, grated cheese, basil, sunflower kernels and garlic in a blender; cover and process until blended.

2. In a large skillet, heat remaining oil over medium-high heat. Add the chopped red pepper; cook and stir until tender. Add corn and pesto; heat through.

3. Halve peppers lengthwise; remove seeds. Grill peppers, covered, over medium heat, cut side down, 8 minutes. Turn; fill with the corn mixture. Grill 4-6 minutes longer or until tender. If desired, sprinkle with shredded cheese.

1 STUFFED PEPPER HALF: 287 cal., 19g fat (4g sat. fat), 6mg chol., 168mg sod., 26g carb. (4g sugars, 4g fiber), 7g pro.

TEST KITCHEN TIP

Use various colored sweet peppers—red, yellow, orange, green or purple—for a beautiful presentation for any summer barbecue party.

GRILLED PATTYPANS

Just a few minutes and a handful of items are all you'll need for this scrumptious side dish. Hoisin sauce and rice wine vinegar add a touch of Asian style.
—*Taste of Home* Test Kitchen

TAKES: 15 min. • **MAKES:** 6 servings

6 cups pattypan squash (about 1½ lbs.)
¼ cup apricot spreadable fruit
2 tsp. hoisin sauce
1 tsp. rice vinegar
½ tsp. sesame oil
¼ tsp. salt
⅛ tsp. ground ginger

1. Place squash in a grill wok or basket coated with cooking spray. Grill, covered, over medium heat until tender, 4 minutes on each side.

2. Meanwhile, in a small bowl, combine the remaining ingredients. Transfer squash to a serving bowl; add sauce and toss gently.

NOTE: If you do not have a grill wok or basket, use a disposable foil pan. Poke holes in the bottom of the pan with a meat fork to allow any liquid to drain.

¾ CUP: 54 cal., 0 fat (0 sat. fat), 0 chol., 127mg sod., 12g carb. (8g sugars, 1g fiber), 1g pro. **DIABETIC EXCHANGES:** 1 vegetable, ½ starch.

PESTO-CORN PEPPERS

CHEESY GARLIC
HERB QUICK BREAD

BROCCOLI TIMBALES WITH LEMON SAUCE

This side dish comes with a no-fuss lemon sauce, making it a welcome addition to all sorts of meals. Don't have ramekins? Use muffin cups instead.
—Kristin Arnett, Elkhorn, WI

PREP: 20 min. + standing • **BAKE:** 25 min.
MAKES: 6 servings

- 1½ cups heavy whipping cream, divided
- 2 Tbsp. lemon juice
- 3 large eggs
- 3 large egg yolks
- 6 oz. cream cheese, softened
- 5 Tbsp. butter, softened, divided
- 2 to 3 Tbsp. grated Parmesan cheese
- 4 cups chopped fresh broccoli (about 1¼ lbs.)
- ½ tsp. salt, divided
- ¼ tsp. white pepper, divided
- 1 Tbsp. all-purpose flour
- 1 tsp. chicken bouillon granules
- 3 Tbsp. snipped fresh dill
  Fresh dill sprigs, optional

1. In a small bowl, combine 1 cup cream and the lemon juice; let stand for 1 hour at room temperature. Place the remaining cream in a blender. Add the eggs, egg yolks, cream cheese, 4 Tbsp. butter and cheese; cover and process until blended. Transfer mixture to a large bowl; fold in the broccoli, ¼ tsp. salt and ⅛ tsp. pepper.
2. Divide broccoli mixture among six 6-oz. ramekins. Place cups in a baking pan. Fill pan with boiling water to a depth of 1 in. Bake, uncovered, at 350° until a knife inserted in the center comes out clean, 25-30 minutes.
3. For sauce, combine flour and remaining butter to form a paste. In a large, heavy saucepan, combine lemon-cream mixture, chicken bouillon and the remaining salt and pepper. Bring to boil. Whisk butter mixture into cream mixture until smooth and mixture is thickened. Add snipped dill. Remove from the heat and set aside.
4. Carefully run a knife around the edge of each custard cup to loosen. Invert onto individual serving plates. Spoon sauce around each timbale; if desired, garnish with dill sprigs.
1 TIMBALE: 434 cal., 42g fat (25g sat. fat), 337mg chol., 577mg sod., 7g carb. (4g sugars, 1g fiber), 9g pro.

CHEESY GARLIC HERB QUICK BREAD

Using sharp cheddar cheese, we think we created the perfect skillet bread for any menu. It's a tasty, easy and fun way to use your cast iron skillet.
—*Taste of Home* Test Kitchen

PREP: 15 min. • **BAKE:** 25 min.
MAKES: 1 loaf (12 slices)

- 3 cups all-purpose flour
- 3 Tbsp. sugar
- 2 tsp. Italian seasoning
- 1 tsp. garlic powder
- ½ tsp. salt
- 1 large egg
- 1 cup fat-free milk
- ⅓ cup canola oil
- 1 cup shredded sharp cheddar cheese

1. Preheat oven to 350°. In a large bowl, whisk together first five ingredients. In another bowl, whisk together egg, milk and oil. Stir in cheese and add to flour mixture; stir just until moistened.
2. Spoon batter into a greased 9-in. cast-iron skillet and bake at 350° until a toothpick inserted in the center comes out clean, 25-30 minutes.
1 SLICE: 233 cal., 10g fat (2g sat. fat), 25mg chol., 175mg sod., 29g carb. (4g sugars, 1g fiber), 7g pro.

KATHY'S HERBED CORN

My husband and I agreed that the original recipe for this corn needed a little jazzing up, so I added thyme and cayenne pepper to suit our tastes. Now fresh corn makes a regular appearance at our place.
—Kathy VonKorff, North College Hill, OH

TAKES: 30 min. • **MAKES:** 8 servings

½ cup butter, softened
2 Tbsp. minced fresh parsley
2 Tbsp. minced fresh chives
1 tsp. dried thyme
½ tsp. salt
½ tsp. cayenne pepper
8 ears sweet corn, husked

1. In a small bowl, beat the first six ingredients until blended. Spread 1 Tbsp. mixture over each ear of corn. Wrap corn individually in heavy-duty foil.
2. Grill corn, covered, over medium heat 10-15 minutes or until tender, turning occasionally. Open foil carefully to allow steam to escape.
1 EAR OF CORN: 179 cal., 12g fat (7g sat. fat), 31mg chol., 277mg sod., 17g carb. (5g sugars, 3g fiber), 3g pro.

PARMESAN & GARLIC FRIES

We found an even tastier way to eat fries! The addition of Parmesan and garlic makes this side dish simple irresistible.
—*Taste of Home* Test Kitchen

TAKES: 20 min. • **MAKES:** 5 servings

5 cups frozen French-fried potatoes
2 Tbsp. olive oil
3 to 4 garlic cloves, minced
¼ tsp. salt
¼ cup grated Parmesan cheese

1. Preheat oven to 450°. Place potatoes in a large bowl. Mix oil, garlic and salt; toss with potatoes. Arrange in a single layer on a large baking sheet.
2. Bake 15-20 minutes or until golden brown, stirring once. Sprinkle with cheese; toss lightly. Serve immediately.
1 SERVING: 199 cal., 11g fat (2g sat. fat), 4mg chol., 524mg sod., 18g carb. (1g sugars, 2g fiber), 4g pro.

SPICY REFRIED BEANS

SPICY REFRIED BEANS

We love the idea of jazzing up refried beans with jalapeno pepper, seasonings and cheese. Serve with tortilla chips on the side.
—*Taste of Home* Test Kitchen

TAKES: 15 min. • **MAKES:** 2 cups

1 small onion, chopped
1 jalapeno pepper, seeded and chopped
1 garlic clove, minced
2 tsp. vegetable oil
1 can (16 oz.) refried beans
2 Tbsp. water
1 tsp. hot pepper sauce
¼ tsp. ground cumin
¼ tsp. chili powder
⅛ tsp. cayenne pepper
½ cup shredded Monterey Jack cheese

In a large skillet, saute the onion, jalapeno and garlic in oil for 2-3 minutes or until tender. Stir in the beans, water, hot pepper sauce, cumin, chili powder and cayenne. Cook and stir over medium-low heat until heated through. Transfer to a serving bowl; sprinkle with cheese.
NOTE: Wear disposable gloves when cutting hot peppers; the oils can burn skin. Avoid touching your face.
¼ CUP: 95 cal., 4g fat (2g sat. fat), 11mg chol., 212mg sod., 10g carb. (2g sugars, 3g fiber), 5g pro. **DIABETIC EXCHANGES:** 1 fat, ½ starch.

ROSEMARY ROOT VEGETABLES

This heartwarming side dish is sure to get rave reviews! Although the ingredient list may look long, you'll soon see that the colorful fall medley is a snap to prepare.
—*Taste of Home* Test Kitchen

PREP: 20 min. • **BAKE:** 20 min.
MAKES: 10 servings

- 1 small rutabaga, peeled and chopped
- 1 medium sweet potato, peeled and chopped
- 2 medium parsnips, peeled and chopped
- 1 medium turnip, peeled and chopped
- ¼ lb. fresh Brussels sprouts, halved
- 2 Tbsp. olive oil
- 2 Tbsp. minced fresh rosemary or 2 tsp. dried rosemary, crushed
- 1 tsp. minced garlic
- ½ tsp. salt
- ½ tsp. pepper

Preheat oven to 425°. Place vegetables in a large bowl. In a small bowl, combine oil, rosemary, garlic, salt and pepper. Pour over vegetables; toss to coat. Arrange vegetables in a single layer in two 15x10x1-in. baking pans coated with cooking spray. Bake, uncovered, stirring once, until tender, 20-25 minutes.

¾ CUP: 78 cal., 3g fat (0 sat. fat), 0 chol., 137mg sod., 13g carb. (5g sugars, 3g fiber), 1g pro. **DIABETIC EXCHANGES:** 1 starch, ½ fat.

SLOW-COOKER CREAMED CORN WITH BACON

SLOW-COOKER CREAMED CORN WITH BACON

Every time we take this rich side dish to a potluck or work party, we leave with an empty slow cooker. It's decadent yet homey, and it goes with everything.
—Melissa Pelkey Hass, Waleska, GA

PREP: 10 min. • **COOK:** 4 hours
MAKES: 20 servings (½ cup each)

- 10 cups frozen corn (about 50 oz.), thawed
- 3 pkg. (8 oz. each) cream cheese, cubed
- ½ cup 2% milk
- ½ cup heavy whipping cream
- ½ cup butter, melted
- ¼ cup sugar
- 2 tsp. salt
- ¼ tsp. pepper
- 4 bacon strips, cooked and crumbled
Chopped green onions

In a 5-qt. slow cooker, combine the first eight ingredients. Cook, covered, on low 4-5 hours or until heated through. Stir just before serving. Sprinkle with the bacon and chopped green onions.

½ CUP: 259 cal., 20g fat (11g sat. fat), 60mg chol., 433mg sod., 18g carb. (6g sugars, 1g fiber), 5g pro.

GREAT GARLIC BREAD

Our tasty garlic bread topped with cheese adds wow to any pasta entree.
—*Taste of Home* Test Kitchen

TAKES: 15 min. • **MAKES:** 8 servings

- ½ cup butter, melted
- ¼ cup grated Romano cheese
- 4 garlic cloves, minced
- 1 loaf (1 lb.) French bread, halved lengthwise
- 2 Tbsp. minced fresh parsley

1. Preheat oven to 350°. In a small bowl, mix butter, cheese and garlic; brush over cut sides of bread. Place on a baking sheet, cut side up. Sprinkle with parsley.

2. Bake 7-9 minutes or until light golden brown. Cut into slices; serve warm.

1 SLICE: 283 cal., 14g fat (8g sat. fat), 34mg chol., 457mg sod., 33g carb. (1g sugars, 1g fiber), 8g pro.

READER RAVE

"This is the recipe I've been using for years. It's a simple garlic bread that's always a hit."
—CRANDCBRUNS, TASTEOFHOME.COM

AMISH ONION CAKE

This change-of-pace bread with an onion-poppy seed topping is a wonderful break from the everyday bread routine. It's a nice accompaniment to soup or salad. I've baked it many times, and I am often asked to share the recipe.
—Mitzi Sentiff, Annapolis, MD

PREP: 25 min. • **BAKE:** 35 min.
MAKES: 12 servings

- 3 to 4 medium onions, chopped
- 2 cups cold butter, divided
- 1 Tbsp. poppy seeds
- 1½ tsp. salt
- 1½ tsp. paprika
- 1 tsp. coarsely ground pepper
- 4 cups all-purpose flour
- ½ cup cornstarch
- 1 Tbsp. baking powder
- 1 Tbsp. sugar
- 1 Tbsp. brown sugar
- 5 large eggs
- ¾ cup 2% milk
- ¾ cup sour cream

1. In a large skillet, cook onions in ½ cup butter over low heat for 10 minutes. Stir in the poppy seeds, salt, paprika and pepper; cook until onions are golden brown, stirring occasionally. Remove from heat; set aside.

2. In a large bowl, combine the flour, cornstarch, baking powder and sugars. Cut in 1¼ cups butter until mixture resembles coarse crumbs. Melt the remaining butter. In a small bowl, whisk the eggs, milk, sour cream and melted butter. Make a well in the dry ingredients; stir in egg mixture just until moistened.

3. Spread into a greased 10-in. springform pan or 10-in. cast-iron skillet. Spoon onion mixture over the batter. Place pan on a baking sheet. Bake at 350° until a toothpick inserted in the center comes out clean, 35-40 minutes. Serve warm.

1 PIECE: 539 cal., 36g fat (22g sat. fat), 182mg chol., 748mg sod., 44g carb. (7g sugars, 2g fiber), 9g pro.

LEMON RICE PILAF

No need to buy premade pilaf mix when you can easily make your own in 20 minutes. We found that a bit of lemon zest adds a lovely burst of flavor.
—*Taste of Home* Test Kitchen

TAKES: 20 min. • **MAKES:** 6 servings

- 1 cup uncooked jasmine or long grain white rice
- 2 Tbsp. butter
- 1 cup sliced celery
- 1 cup thinly sliced green onions
- 1 Tbsp. grated lemon zest
- 1 tsp. salt
- ¼ tsp. pepper

Cook rice according to package directions. Meanwhile, in a large skillet, heat butter over medium heat. Add celery and onions; cook until tender. Add rice, lemon zest, salt and pepper; toss lightly. Cook until heated through.

¾ CUP: 155 cal., 4g fat (2g sat. fat), 10mg chol., 454mg sod., 27g carb. (1g sugars, 1g fiber), 3g pro.

AMISH ONION CAKE

CAULIFLOWER WITH ROASTED ALMOND & PEPPER DIP

CAULIFLOWER WITH ROASTED ALMOND & PEPPER DIP

Make cauliflower sing with this sauce, rich in both color and flavor. The sauce takes some time but is well worth it.
—Lauren Knoelke, Des Moines, IA

PREP: 40 min. • **BAKE:** 35 min.
MAKES: 10 servings (2¼ cups dip)

- 10 cups water
- 1 cup olive oil, divided
- ¾ cup sherry or red wine vinegar, divided
- 3 Tbsp. salt
- 1 bay leaf
- 1 Tbsp. crushed red pepper flakes
- 1 large head cauliflower
- ½ cup whole almonds, toasted
- ½ cup soft whole wheat or white bread crumbs, toasted
- ½ cup fire-roasted crushed tomatoes
- 1 jar (8 oz.) roasted sweet red peppers, drained
- 2 Tbsp. minced fresh parsley
- 2 garlic cloves
- 1 tsp. sweet paprika
- ½ tsp. salt
- ¼ tsp. freshly ground pepper

1. In a 6-qt. stockpot, bring water, ½ cup oil, ½ cup sherry, salt, bay leaf and pepper flakes to a boil. Add the cauliflower. Reduce heat; simmer, uncovered, until a knife easily inserts into center, 15-20 minutes, turning halfway through cooking. Remove with a slotted spoon; drain well on paper towels.

2. Preheat oven to 450°. Place cauliflower on a greased wire rack in a 15x10x1-in. baking pan. Bake on a lower oven rack until dark golden, 35-40 minutes.

3. Meanwhile, place almonds, bread crumbs, tomatoes, roasted peppers, parsley, garlic, paprika, salt and pepper in a food processor; pulse until finely chopped. Add remaining sherry; process until blended. Continue processing while gradually adding remaining oil in a steady stream. Serve with cauliflower.

1 SERVING: 194 cal., 16g fat (2g sat. fat), 0 chol., 470mg sod., 9g carb. (3g sugars, 3g fiber), 4g pro.

HERBED DINNER ROLLS

HERBED DINNER ROLLS

To dress up everyday dinner rolls, brush herbed butter over the dough, then form accordion rolls. The aroma is incredible!
—*Taste of Home* Test Kitchen

PREP: 40 min. + rising • **BAKE:** 20 min.
MAKES: 2 dozen

- 2 pkg. (¼ oz. each) active dry yeast
- ½ cup warm water (110° to 115°)
- 1 tsp. plus ⅓ cup sugar, divided
- 1¼ cups warm 2% milk (110° to 115°)
- ½ cup butter, melted
- 2 large eggs, room temperature
- 1½ tsp. salt
- 6 to 6½ cups all-purpose flour
- 3 Tbsp. butter, softened
- 1 tsp. Italian seasoning
- 1 large egg white, beaten

1. In a large bowl, dissolve yeast in warm water with 1 tsp. sugar. Add milk, melted butter, eggs, salt, 3 cups flour and remaining sugar; beat until smooth. Stir in enough remaining flour to form a soft dough.

2. Turn onto a floured surface; knead until smooth and elastic, about 6-8 minutes. Place in a greased bowl, turning once to grease the top. Cover and let rise in a warm place until doubled, about 1 hour.

3. Punch dough down; place on a lightly floured surface. Divide into four portions. Roll each portion into a 14x6-in. rectangle. Combine softened butter and Italian seasoning; spread over dough.

4. Score each rectangle widthwise at 2-in. intervals. Using marks as a guide, fold dough accordion-style back and forth along score lines. Cut folded dough into six 1-in. pieces. Place pieces cut side down in greased muffin cups. Cover and let rise until doubled, about 30 minutes.

5. Preheat oven to 375°. Uncover and let stand another 10 minutes before baking. Brush with egg white. Bake until golden brown, 18-22 minutes. Remove from pans to wire racks.

1 ROLL: 186 cal., 6g fat (4g sat. fat), 32mg chol., 200mg sod., 28g carb. (4g sugars, 1g fiber), 5g pro. **DIABETIC EXCHANGES:** 1½ starch, 1 fat.

BASIL & OREGANO DINNER ROLLS: Substitute ½ tsp. each dried oregano and basil for Italian seasoning.

FRESH HERB DINNER ROLLS: Substitute 1½ tsp. minced fresh parsley and ½ tsp. minced fresh thyme for the Italian seasoning.

WALNUT ZUCCHINI MUFFINS

Shredded zucchini adds moisture to these tender muffins dotted with raisins and chopped walnuts. If you have a surplus of zucchini in summer as many of us do, this is a tasty way to use some of it.
—Harriet Stichter, Milford, IN

PREP: 20 min. • **BAKE:** 20 min.
MAKES: 1 dozen

- 1   cup all-purpose flour
- ¾   cup whole wheat flour
- ⅔   cup packed brown sugar
- 2   tsp. baking powder
- ¾   tsp. ground cinnamon
- ½   tsp. salt
- 2   large eggs
- ¾   cup 2% milk
- ½   cup butter, melted
- 1   cup shredded zucchini
- 1   cup chopped walnuts
- ½   cup raisins

1. Preheat oven to 375°. In a large bowl, whisk the first six ingredients. In another bowl, whisk eggs, milk and melted butter until blended. Add to flour mixture; stir just until moistened. Fold in zucchini, walnuts and raisins.

2. Fill 12 greased muffin cups three-fourths full. Bake 18-20 minutes or until a toothpick inserted in center comes out clean. Cool for 5 minutes before removing from pan to a wire rack. Serve warm.

FREEZE OPTION: Freeze cooled muffins in sealed freezer containers. To use, thaw at room temperature or, if desired, microwave each muffin on high until heated through, 20-30 seconds.

1 MUFFIN: 281 cal., 15g fat (6g sat. fat), 53mg chol., 250mg sod., 33g carb. (17g sugars, 2g fiber), 6g pro.

PRETTY DUCHESS POTATOES

Comfort-food flavor comes in attractive packages that are just the right size!
—*Taste of Home* Test Kitchen

PREP: 35 min. • **BAKE:** 20 min.
MAKES: 6 servings

- 2   lbs. russet potatoes, peeled and quartered
- 3   large egg yolks
- 3   Tbsp. fat-free milk
- 2   Tbsp. butter
- 1   tsp. salt
- ¼   tsp. pepper
- ⅛   tsp. ground nutmeg
- 1   large egg, lightly beaten

1. Place potatoes in a large saucepan and cover with water. Bring to a boil. Reduce heat; cover and simmer 15-20 minutes or until tender. Drain. Over very low heat, stir potatoes 1-2 minutes or until steam has evaporated. Remove from heat.

2. Preheat oven to 400°. Press potatoes through a potato ricer or strainer into a large bowl. Stir in the egg yolks, milk, butter, salt, pepper and nutmeg.

3. Using a pastry bag or heavy-duty resealable plastic bag and a large star tip, pipe potatoes into six mounds on a parchment-lined baking sheet. Brush with beaten egg. Bake 20-25 minutes or until golden brown.

1 SERVING: 158 cal., 7g fat (3g sat. fat), 134mg chol., 437mg sod., 21g carb. (2g sugars, 1g fiber), 4g pro. **DIABETIC EXCHANGES:** 1½ fat, 1 starch.

WALNUT ZUCCHINI MUFFINS

CILANTRO GINGER CARROTS

COLORFUL COUSCOUS

We love it when plain side dishes get a tiny pop of color, like the bright pepper accents you'll see in this light and fluffy couscous. It's a scrumptious and welcome switch from baked potatoes or rice.
—*Taste of Home* Test Kitchen

TAKES: 25 min. • **MAKES:** 6 servings

- 2 Tbsp. olive oil
- 5 miniature sweet peppers, julienned
- ⅓ cup finely chopped onion
- 2 garlic cloves, minced
- 1 can (14½ oz.) chicken broth
- ¼ cup water
- ½ tsp. salt
- ¼ tsp. pepper
- 1 pkg. (10 oz.) couscous

In a large saucepan, heat oil over medium-high heat; saute peppers, onion and garlic until tender, 2-3 minutes. Stir in broth, water, salt and pepper; bring to a boil. Stir in couscous. Remove from heat; let stand, covered, 5 minutes. Fluff with a fork.
¾ CUP: 220 cal., 5g fat (1g sat. fat), 2mg chol., 498mg sod., 37g carb. (2g sugars, 2g fiber), 7g pro.

CILANTRO GINGER CARROTS

Peppery-sweet ginger and cooling cilantro have starring roles in this colorful side of crisp-tender carrots. They go from pan to plate in no time flat.
—*Taste of Home* Test Kitchen

TAKES: 15 min. • **MAKES:** 4 servings

- 1 Tbsp. butter
- 1 lb. fresh carrots, sliced diagonally
- 1½ tsp. minced fresh gingerroot
- 2 Tbsp. chopped fresh cilantro
- ½ tsp. salt
- ¼ tsp. pepper

In a large skillet, heat butter over medium-high heat. Add carrots; cook and stir until crisp-tender, 4-6 minutes. Add ginger; cook 1 minute longer. Stir in cilantro, salt and pepper.
½ CUP: 73 cal., 3g fat (2g sat. fat), 8mg chol., 396mg sod., 11g carb. (5g sugars, 3g fiber), 1g pro. **DIABETIC EXCHANGES:** 1 vegetable, ½ fat.

ROASTED BEET WEDGES

This recipe makes ordinary beets taste tender and delicious with just a few sweet and good-for-you ingredients.
—Wendy Stenman, Germantown, WI

PREP: 15 min. • **BAKE:** 1 hour
MAKES: 4 servings

- 1 lb. medium fresh beets, peeled
- 4 tsp. olive oil
- ½ tsp. kosher salt
- 3 to 5 fresh rosemary sprigs

1. Preheat oven to 400°. Cut each beet into six wedges; place in a shallow dish. Add olive oil and salt; toss gently to coat.
2. Place a piece of heavy-duty foil about 12 in. long in a 15x10x1-in. baking pan. Arrange beets on foil; top with rosemary. Fold foil around beets and seal tightly.
3. Bake until tender, about 1 hour. Open foil carefully to allow steam to escape. Discard rosemary sprigs.
3 WEDGES: 92 cal., 5g fat (1g sat. fat), 0 chol., 328mg sod., 12g carb. (9g sugars, 3g fiber), 2g pro. **DIABETIC EXCHANGES:** 1 vegetable, 1 fat.

DIPPED GINGERSNAPS
PAGE 95

Cookies, Brownies & Bars

It's snack time, and the team at *Taste of Home* has filled the cookie jar with nothing but the best-of-the-best bites. Turn here for 18 sensational sweets, potluck greats and classroom treats bound to become favorites in your home for years to come.

CINNAMON BROWNIES

For Christmas one year, a friend gave us a pan of these delicious brownies. Before I figured out the secret ingredient was cinnamon, half the pan was already gone!
—Gail Mehle, Rock Springs, WY

PREP: 20 min. • **BAKE:** 40 min. + cooling
MAKES: 3 dozen

- ¾ cup baking cocoa
- ½ tsp. baking soda
- ⅔ cup butter, melted, divided
- ½ cup boiling water
- 2 cups sugar
- 2 large eggs, beaten, room temperature
- 1 tsp. vanilla extract
- 1⅓ cups all-purpose flour
- 1½ to 2 tsp. ground cinnamon
- ¼ tsp. salt
- 1 cup (6 oz.) semisweet chocolate chips

FROSTING
- 6 Tbsp. butter, softened
- ½ cup baking cocoa
- 2⅔ cups confectioners' sugar
- 1 to 1½ tsp. ground cinnamon
- ⅓ cup evaporated milk
- 1 tsp. vanilla extract

1. In a bowl, combine cocoa and baking soda; blend in ⅓ cup melted butter. Add boiling water, stirring until thickened. Stir in sugar, eggs, vanilla and remaining butter. Add flour, cinnamon and salt. Fold in chocolate chips. Pour into a greased 13x9-in. baking pan. Bake at 350° for 40 minutes or until brownies test done. Cool.
2. For frosting, cream butter in a bowl. Combine cocoa, sugar and cinnamon; add alternately with the milk. Beat to a spreading consistency; add vanilla. Add more milk if necessary. Spread over the brownies.
1 BROWNIE: 137 cal., 7g fat (4g sat. fat), 27mg chol., 94mg sod., 17g carb. (11g sugars, 1g fiber), 2g pro.

TOFFEE-CHIP SUGAR COOKIES

TOFFEE-CHIP SUGAR COOKIES

When you taste these chewy cookies, you won't believe they call for only two ingredients! Keep the makings on hand so you can bake them upon request.
—*Taste of Home* Test Kitchen

TAKES: 20 min. • **MAKES:** about 2½ dozen

- 1 tube (18 oz.) refrigerated sugar cookie dough
- 4 Heath candy bars (1.4 oz. each), finely chopped

1. Slice the cookie dough into ¼-in. slices. Place 2 in. apart on lightly greased baking sheets. Sprinkle each dough circle with 2 tsp. chopped candy bars.
2. Bake at 350° for 7-9 minutes or until the edges are lightly browned. Remove to wire racks to cool.

1 COOKIE: 81 cal., 4g fat (1g sat. fat), 5mg chol., 75mg sod., 11g carb. (5g sugars, 0 fiber), 1g pro.
SUREFIRE SUGAR COOKIES: Slice and bake sugar cookies according to package directions; cool. Melt 1½ cups semisweet chocolate chips with 4½ tsp. shortening; stir until smooth. Dip cookies halfway in melted chocolate. Place on waxed paper; immediately sprinkle with colored sprinkles, chopped nuts or flaked coconut. Let stand until set.
PECAN-TOPPED SUGAR COOKIES: Beat one 8-oz. can almond paste with 3 oz. softened cream cheese; stir in ¼ cup flaked coconut. Cut cookie dough into ½-in. slices; divide each slice into four portions. Place on baking sheets as directed. Top each with ½ tsp. almond mixture and one pecan half. Bake 10-12 minutes; cool.

FIVE-CHIP COOKIES

With peanut butter, oats and five kinds of chips, these quick cookies make a hearty snack that appeals to kids of all ages. I sometimes double the recipe to share.
—Sharon Hedstrom, Minnetonka, MN

- -

PREP: 25 min. • **BAKE:** 10 min./batch
MAKES: 4½ dozen

1	cup butter, softened
1	cup peanut butter
1	cup sugar
⅔	cup packed brown sugar
2	large eggs
1	tsp. vanilla extract
2	cups all-purpose flour
1	cup old-fashioned oats
2	tsp. baking soda
½	tsp. salt
⅔	cup each milk chocolate chips, semisweet chocolate chips, peanut butter chips, white baking chips and butterscotch chips

1. Preheat oven to 350°. In a large bowl, cream butter, peanut butter and sugars until light and fluffy. Add the eggs, one at a time, beating well after each addition. Beat in vanilla. Combine flour, oats, baking soda and salt; gradually add to creamed mixture and mix well. Stir in chips.
2. Drop by rounded tablespoonfuls 2 in. apart onto ungreased baking sheets. Bake 10-12 minutes or until lightly browned. Cool 1 minute before removing to wire racks.
NOTE: Reduced-fat peanut butter is not recommended for this recipe.
1 COOKIE: 168 cal., 10g fat (5g sat. fat), 17mg chol., 130mg sod., 19g carb. (13g sugars, 1g fiber), 3g pro.

READER RAVE

"Oh, my goodness! These are truly out of this world. My husband grabs them while they're still warm out of oven. He's been known to eat a half-dozen at a time."

—JOSCY, TASTEOFHOME.COM

DOUBLE BUTTERSCOTCH COOKIES

DOUBLE BUTTERSCOTCH COOKIES

I've baked up this old-fashioned recipe for years. It can also be made with miniature chocolate chips or coconut in place of the toffee bits if you'd like.
—Beverly Duncan, Lakeville, OH

- -

PREP: 20 min. + chilling
BAKE: 10 min./batch + cooling
MAKES: about 7 dozen

½	cup butter, softened
½	cup shortening
4	cups packed brown sugar
4	large eggs
1	Tbsp. vanilla extract
6	cups all-purpose flour
3	tsp. baking soda
3	tsp. cream of tartar
1	tsp. salt
1	pkg. English toffee bits (10 oz.) or almond brickle chips (7½ oz.)
1	cup finely chopped pecans

1. In a large bowl, beat butter, shortening and brown sugar for 2 minutes or until mixture resembles wet sand. Add eggs, one at a time, beating well after each addition. Beat in vanilla. Combine the flour, baking soda, cream of tartar and salt; gradually add to the brown sugar mixture and mix well. Stir in toffee bits and pecans.
2. Shape into three 14-in. rolls (mixture will be slightly crumbly); wrap each in plastic. Refrigerate for 4 hours or until firm.
3. Unwrap and cut into ½-in. slices. Place 2 in. apart on greased baking sheets. Bake at 375° until lightly browned, 9-11 minutes. Cool for 1-2 minutes before removing from pans to wire racks to cool completely.
2 COOKIES: 248 cal., 9g fat (3g sat. fat), 28mg chol., 221mg sod., 39g carb. (25g sugars, 1g fiber), 3g pro.

VALENTINE HEART BROWNIES

Steal hearts on Valentine's Day with brownies that have cute, yummy frosting centers. They are simply irresistible.
—*Taste of Home* Test Kitchen

PREP: 35 min. • **BAKE:** 20 min. + cooling
MAKES: 15 servings

- 1 pkg. fudge brownie mix (13x9-in. pan size)
- ¼ tsp. mint extract
- ½ cup butter, softened
- 1½ cups confectioners' sugar
- ¼ tsp. vanilla extract
  Red paste food coloring, optional
- ¼ cup baking cocoa

1. Prepare brownie mix according to package directions, adding mint extract to batter. Transfer to a greased 13x9-in. baking pan. Bake at 350° for 20-25 minutes or until a toothpick inserted in the center comes out clean. Cool completely on a wire rack.

2. Meanwhile, in a small bowl, cream the butter, confectioners' sugar, vanilla and, if desired, food coloring until light and fluffy.

Place in a heavy-duty resealable plastic bag; cut a small hole in a corner of bag. Set aside.

3. Line a baking sheet with parchment. Dust with cocoa; set aside. Cut brownies into 15 rectangles. Using a 1½-in. heart-shaped cookie cutter, cut out a heart from the center of each brownie. Reserve cutout centers for another use. Place brownies on prepared baking sheet. Pipe frosting into centers of brownies.

1 BROWNIE: 334 cal., 18g fat (6g sat. fat), 42mg chol., 201mg sod., 41g carb. (30g sugars, 1g fiber), 3g pro.

CHOCOLATE CARAMEL THUMBPRINTS

Covered in chopped nuts and drizzled with chocolate, these cookies are as delicious as they are pretty. At my house, everybody looks forward to munching on them.
—Elizabeth Marino,
San Juan Capistrano, CA

PREP: 25 min. + chilling
BAKE: 10 min./batch
MAKES: about 2½ dozen

- ½ cup butter, softened
- ⅔ cup sugar
- 1 large egg, separated, room temperature
- 2 Tbsp. 2% milk
- 1 tsp. vanilla extract
- 1 cup all-purpose flour
- ⅓ cup baking cocoa
- ¼ tsp. salt
- 1 cup finely chopped pecans

FILLING
- 12 to 14 caramels
- 3 Tbsp. heavy whipping cream
- ½ cup semisweet chocolate chips
- 1 tsp. shortening

1. In a large bowl, cream butter and sugar until light and fluffy. Beat in egg yolk, milk and vanilla. In another bowl, whisk flour, cocoa and salt; gradually beat into creamed mixture. Refrigerate, covered, 1 hour or until easy to handle.

2. Preheat oven to 350°. Shape dough into 1-in. balls. In a shallow bowl, beat egg white. Place pecans in a separate shallow bowl. Dip balls in egg white, then in pecans, patting to help pecans adhere.

3. Place 2 in. apart on greased baking sheets. Press a deep indentation in center of each with the end of a wooden spoon handle. Bake 10-12 minutes or until set. Remove from pans to wire racks to cool.

4. In a large heavy saucepan, melt caramels with cream over low heat; stir until smooth. Fill each cookie with about ½ tsp. caramel mixture. In a microwave, melt chocolate chips and shortening; stir until smooth. Drizzle over cookies; let stand until set. Store in an airtight container.

1 COOKIE: 128 cal., 8g fat (3g sat. fat), 17mg chol., 55mg sod., 14g carb. (9g sugars, 1g fiber), 2g pro.

VALENTINE HEART BROWNIES

PUMPKIN PIE BARS

BLACK FOREST ICEBOX COOKIES

These rich chocolate wafers are the perfect complement to the creamy filling's sweet-tart tones. Chill for up to four hours; any longer and the wafers become a bit too soft to pick up with your hands.
—*Taste of Home* Test Kitchen

- -

PREP: 15 min. + chilling
COOK: 5 min. + cooling
MAKES: 20 cookies

- 3 Tbsp. sugar
- 4 tsp. cornstarch
  Dash salt
- ¾ cup fresh or frozen pitted tart cherries (thawed), coarsely chopped
- ¾ cup cherry juice blend
- 1½ tsp. lemon juice
- 1 to 2 drops red food coloring, optional
- ½ cup mascarpone cheese
- 1 Tbsp. confectioners' sugar
- 1 tsp. cherry brandy
- 1 pkg. (9 oz.) chocolate wafers
- ½ cup semisweet chocolate chips
- ¼ cup heavy whipping cream

1. In a small saucepan, combine the granulated sugar, cornstarch and salt. Add the cherries, juice blend and lemon juice. Bring to a boil; cook and stir for 2 minutes or until thickened. Remove from the heat and stir in food coloring if desired. Cool to room temperature.
2. In a small bowl, combine the mascarpone cheese, confectioners' sugar and brandy. Spread about 1 tsp. cheese mixture onto each of 20 wafers; layer each with 2 tsp. cherry mixture. Top with remaining wafers. Place on a waxed paper-lined baking pan. Place chocolate chips in a small bowl. In a small saucepan, bring cream just to a boil. Pour over chips; whisk until smooth. Drizzle over cookies. Refrigerate, covered, for up to 4 hours before serving.
1 SANDWICH COOKIE: 139 cal., 9g fat (4g sat. fat), 17mg chol., 81mg sod., 15g carb. (9g sugars, 1g fiber), 2g pro.

PUMPKIN PIE BARS

These heartwarming bars taste like a cross between pumpkin pie and pecan pie.
—Sue Draheim, Waterford, WI

- -

PREP: 15 min. • **BAKE:** 50 min. + chilling
MAKES: 16 servings

- 1 can (29 oz.) solid-pack pumpkin
- 1 can (12 oz.) evaporated milk
- 1½ cups sugar
- 4 large eggs
- 2 tsp. ground cinnamon
- 1 tsp. ground ginger
- ½ tsp. ground nutmeg
- 1 pkg. butter recipe golden cake mix (regular size)
- 1 cup butter, melted
- 1 cup chopped pecans
  Whipped topping, optional

1. Preheat oven to 350°. In a large bowl, combine the first seven ingredients; beat on medium speed until smooth. Pour into an ungreased 13x9-in. baking pan. Sprinkle with dry cake mix. Drizzle butter over top; sprinkle with pecans.
2. Bake 50-60 minutes or until a toothpick inserted in center comes out clean. Cool 1 hour on a wire rack.
3. Refrigerate 3 hours or overnight. Remove from the refrigerator 15 minutes before serving. Cut into bars. If desired, serve with whipped topping.
1 BAR: 419 cal., 22g fat (10g sat. fat), 91mg chol., 360mg sod., 53g carb. (38g sugars, 3g fiber), 5g pro.

BLACK FOREST
ICEBOX COOKIES

CHOCOLATE & PEANUT BUTTER CRISPY BARS

To make a dairy-free dessert, I created these sensational bars. My kids and their friends gobble them up. I've written about it on my blog, *joyfulscribblings.com.*
—Dawn Pasco, Overland Park, KS

- -

PREP: 15 min. • **BAKE:** 25 min. + chilling
MAKES: 2 dozen

- 1   pkg. fudge brownie mix (13x9-in. pan size)
- 1½ cups chunky peanut butter
- 2   cups (12 oz.) semisweet chocolate chips
- 1   cup creamy peanut butter
- 3   cups Rice Krispies

1. Line a 13x9-in. baking pan with parchment, letting ends extend up sides. Prepare and bake brownie mix according to package directions, using prepared pan. Cool in the pan on a wire rack for 30 minutes. Refrigerate until cold.

2. Spread chunky peanut butter over chilled brownies. Place chocolate chips and creamy peanut butter in a large microwave-safe bowl. Microwave in 30-second intervals until melted; stir until smooth. Stir in Rice Krispies; spread over chunky peanut butter layer. Refrigerate, covered, at least 30 minutes or until set.

3. Lifting with parchment paper, remove brownies from pan. Cut into bars. Store in an airtight container in the refrigerator.

1 BAR: 390 cal., 27g fat (6g sat. fat), 16mg chol., 234mg sod., 35g carb. (21g sugars, 3g fiber), 9g pro.

S'MORES NO-BAKE COOKIES

There's no easier way to get that familiar s'mores goodness in your kitchen. Mix these cookies together and let them chill until you're ready to share.
—*Taste of Home* Test Kitchen

- -

PREP: 15 min. + chilling • **MAKES:** 2½ dozen

- 1⅔ cups milk chocolate chips
- 2   Tbsp. canola oil
- 3   cups Golden Grahams
- 2   cups miniature marshmallows

In a large microwave-safe bowl, microwave chocolate chips and oil, uncovered, at 50% power for 1-1½ minutes or until chocolate is melted, stirring every 30 seconds. Stir in cereal until blended; fold in marshmallows. Drop by rounded tablespoonfuls onto a waxed paper-lined baking sheet. Refrigerate 15 minutes or until firm.

1 COOKIE: 79 cal., 4g fat (2g sat. fat), 2mg chol., 39mg sod., 11g carb. (8g sugars, 1g fiber), 1g pro.

TEST KITCHEN TIP
Jazz up these no-bake treats by swapping in peanut butter or butterscotch chips for some of the chocolate chips .

CHOCOLATE &
PEANUT BUTTER
CRISPY BARS

RUSTIC NUT BARS

BERRY SHORTBREAD DREAMS

Raspberry jam adds a fruity sweetness to my rich-tasting cookies. They absolutely melt in your mouth, I promise.
—Mildred Sherrer, Fort Worth, TX

PREP: 20 min. + chilling • **BAKE:** 15 min.
MAKES: about 3½ dozen

- 1 cup butter, softened
- ⅔ cup sugar
- ½ tsp. almond extract
- 2 cups all-purpose flour
- ⅓ to ½ cup seedless raspberry jam

GLAZE
- 1 cup confectioners' sugar
- ½ tsp. almond extract
- 2 to 3 tsp. water

1. In a large bowl, cream butter and sugar until light and fluffy. Beat in the extract; gradually add flour until dough forms a ball. Cover and refrigerate for 1 hour or until dough is easy to handle.
2. Roll into 1-in. balls. Place 1 in. apart on ungreased baking sheets. Using the end of a wooden spoon handle, make an indentation in the center. Fill with jam.
3. Bake at 350° for 14-18 minutes or until edges are lightly browned. Remove to wire racks to cool.
4. Spoon additional jam into cookies if desired. Combine confectioners' sugar, extract and enough water to achieve drizzling consistency; drizzle over cookies.
2 COOKIES: 180 cal., 9g fat (5g sat. fat), 23mg chol., 88mg sod., 24g carb. (15g sugars, 0 fiber), 1g pro.

RUSTIC NUT BARS

My friends and I just love crunching into the shortbread-like crust and the wildly nutty topping on these chewy, gooey bars.
—Barbara Driscoll, West Allis, WI

PREP: 20 min. • **BAKE:** 35 min. + cooling
MAKES: about 3 dozen

- 1 Tbsp. plus ¾ cup cold butter, divided
- 2⅓ cups all-purpose flour
- ½ cup sugar
- ½ tsp. baking powder
- ½ tsp. salt
- 1 large egg, lightly beaten, room temperature

TOPPING
- ⅔ cup honey
- ½ cup packed brown sugar
- ¼ tsp. salt
- 6 Tbsp. butter, cubed
- 2 Tbsp. heavy whipping cream
- 1 cup chopped hazelnuts, toasted
- 1 cup salted cashews
- 1 cup pistachios
- 1 cup salted roasted almonds

1. Preheat oven to 375°. Line a 13x9-in. baking pan with foil, letting ends extend over sides by 1 in. Grease foil with 1 Tbsp. butter.
2. In a large bowl, whisk flour, sugar, baking powder and salt. Cut in remaining butter until mixture resembles coarse crumbs. Stir in egg until blended (mixture will be dry). Press firmly onto bottom of prepared pan.
3. Bake 18-20 minutes or until edges are golden brown. Cool on a wire rack.
4. In a large heavy saucepan, combine honey, brown sugar and salt; bring to a boil over medium heat, stirring frequently to dissolve sugar. Boil 2 minutes without stirring. Stir in butter and cream; return to a boil. Cook and stir 1 minute or until smooth. Remove from heat; stir in nuts. Spread over crust.
5. Bake 15-20 minutes or until topping is bubbly. Cool completely in pan on a wire rack. Lifting with foil, remove from pan. Discard foil; cut into bars.
NOTE: To toast nuts, bake in a shallow pan in a 350° oven for 5-10 minutes or cook in a skillet over low heat until lightly browned, stirring occasionally.
1 BAR: 199 cal., 13g fat (4g sat. fat), 21mg chol., 157mg sod., 18g carb. (10g sugars, 1g fiber), 4g pro.

ALMOND-COCONUT
LEMON BARS

ALMOND-COCONUT LEMON BARS

Give traditional lemon bars a tasty twist with the addition of almonds and coconut.
—*Taste of Home* Test Kitchen

PREP: 10 min. • **BAKE:** 40 min. + cooling
MAKES: 2 dozen

- 1½ cups all-purpose flour
- ½ cup confectioners' sugar
- ⅓ cup blanched almonds, toasted
- 1 tsp. grated lemon zest
- ¾ cup cold butter, cubed

FILLING

- 3 large eggs
- 1½ cups sugar
- ½ cup sweetened shredded coconut
- ¼ cup lemon juice
- 3 Tbsp. all-purpose flour
- 1 tsp. grated lemon zest
- ½ tsp. baking powder
  Confectioners' sugar

1. In a food processor, combine the flour, confectioners' sugar, almonds and lemon zest; cover and process until nuts are finely chopped. Add butter; pulse just until mixture is crumbly. Press into a greased 13x9-in. baking pan. Bake at 350° for 20 minutes.
2. Meanwhile, in a large bowl, whisk eggs, sugar, coconut, lemon juice, flour, lemon zest and baking powder; pour over the hot crust. Bake until light golden brown, 20-25 minutes. Cool on a wire rack. Dust with confectioners' sugar. Cut into squares.
1 BAR: 173 cal., 8g fat (5g sat. fat), 39mg chol., 70mg sod., 23g carb. (16g sugars, 1g fiber), 2g pro.

> ### READER RAVE
> *"Made these for a community event and they were gone in a flash. Several people admitted to eating more than one."*
> —SPOOKI03, TASTEOFHOME.COM

DIPPED GINGERSNAPS

DIPPED GINGERSNAPS

I get tremendous satisfaction making and gifting time-tested treats like these soft, chewy cookies. Dipping them in white chocolate makes much-loved gingersnaps even more special.
—Laura Kimball, West Jordan, UT

PREP: 20 min.
BAKE: 10 min./batch + cooling
MAKES: about 14½ dozen

- 2 cups sugar
- 1½ cups canola oil
- 2 large eggs, room temperature
- ½ cup molasses
- 4 cups all-purpose flour
- 4 tsp. baking soda
- 3 tsp. ground ginger
- 2 tsp. ground cinnamon
- 1 tsp. salt
  Additional sugar
- 2 pkg. (10 to 12 oz. each) white baking chips
- ¼ cup shortening

1. In a large bowl, combine sugar and oil. Beat in eggs. Stir in molasses. Combine the flour, baking soda, ginger, cinnamon and salt; gradually add to the creamed mixture and mix well.
2. Shape into ¾-in. balls and roll in sugar. Place 2 in. apart on ungreased baking sheets. Bake at 350° for 10-12 minutes or until cookie springs back when touched lightly. Remove to wire racks to cool.
3. In a microwave, melt chips and shortening; stir until smooth. Dip cookies halfway into the melted chips; allow excess to drip off. Place on waxed paper; let stand until set.
1 COOKIE: 47 cal., 2g fat (0 sat. fat), 2mg chol., 44mg sod., 6g carb. (4g sugars, 0 fiber), 0 pro.

OAT CHOCOLATE CHIP COOKIES

I made this recipe just before we showed our house. Not only did the people buy the house, they requested the recipe! Be sure to try out the variations, too.
—Nancy Fridirici, Brookfield, WI

PREP: 15 min. • **BAKE:** 15 min./batch
MAKES: 4 dozen

- 1 cup butter, softened
- 1 cup sugar
- 1 cup packed brown sugar
- 2 large eggs, room temperature
- 1 tsp. vanilla extract
- 2 cups all-purpose flour
- 1 tsp. baking soda
- ½ tsp. baking powder
- ½ tsp. salt
- 2 cups old-fashioned oats
- 2 cups (12 oz.) semisweet chocolate chips

1. In a large bowl, cream the butter and sugars until light and fluffy. Beat in eggs and vanilla. Combine the flour, baking soda, baking powder and salt; add to creamed mixture and mix well. Stir in the oats and chocolate chips.

2. Drop by rounded tablespoonfuls 2 in. apart onto ungreased baking sheets. Bake at 350° for 11-12 minutes or until golden brown. Cool on wire racks.

1 COOKIE: 135 cal., 6g fat (4g sat. fat), 19mg chol., 88mg sod., 19g carb. (13g sugars, 1g fiber), 2g pro. **DIABETIC EXCHANGES:** 1 starch, 1 fat.

OATMEAL RAISIN COOKIES: Omit chocolate chips. Stir in 1½ cups raisins.

OATMEAL JUMBLE COOKIES: Add 1 tsp. ground cinnamon to flour mixture. Reduce chocolate chips to ¾ cup. Stir in ¾ cup each butterscotch chips, dried cranberries and chopped pecans.

COCONUT OATMEAL COOKIES: Add 1 tsp. ground cinnamon to flour mixture. Reduce chocolate chips to 1¼ cups. Stir in 1 cup chopped pecans and 1 cup flaked coconut.

CHOCOLATE-RAISIN OATMEAL COOKIES: Add ¾ tsp. pumpkin pie spice to flour mixture. Substitute chocolate-covered raisins for the chocolate chips.

MACADAMIA BLOND BROWNIES

MACADAMIA BLOND BROWNIES

Every bite of these blondies is packed with chunks of white and semisweet chocolate and macadamia nuts. They are a potluck offering that always stands out.
—Rosemary Dreiske, Lemmon, SD

PREP: 15 min. • **BAKE:** 25 min. + cooling
MAKES: 2 dozen

- ½ cup butter, softened
- ¾ cup sugar
- ¾ cup packed brown sugar
- 2 large eggs, room temperature
- 2 tsp. vanilla extract
- 1½ cups all-purpose flour
- 1 tsp. baking powder
- ½ tsp. salt
- 1 cup white baking chips
- 1 cup semisweet chocolate chunks
- 1 jar (3 oz.) macadamia nuts or ¾ cup blanched almonds, chopped, divided

1. Preheat oven to 350°. In a large bowl, cream butter and sugars until light and fluffy. Beat in eggs and vanilla. Combine flour, baking powder and salt; gradually add to creamed mixture and mix well. Stir in white chips, chocolate chunks and ½ cup nuts.

2. Spoon into a greased 13x9-in. baking pan; spread over the bottom of pan. Sprinkle with remaining nuts. Bake 25-30 minutes or until top begins to crack and is golden brown. Cool on a wire rack. Cut into bars.

1 BAR: 221 cal., 12g fat (6g sat. fat), 29mg chol., 130mg sod., 28g carb. (17g sugars, 1g fiber), 2g pro.

TEST KITCHEN TIP
This particular brownie batter is very thick, so make sure you spread it evenly in the pan for the best baking results.

RHUBARB CUSTARD BARS

Once I tried these rich, gooey bars, I just had to have the recipe so I could make them for my family and friends. The shortbread-like crust and creamy layers inspire people to find rhubarb they can use to fix a batch for their own families.
—Shari Roach, South Milwaukee, WI

PREP: 25 min. • **BAKE:** 50 min. + chilling
MAKES: 3 dozen

- 2   cups all-purpose flour
- ¼   cup sugar
- 1   cup cold butter

FILLING
- 2   cups sugar
- 7   Tbsp. all-purpose flour
- 1   cup heavy whipping cream
- 3   large eggs, beaten
- 5   cups finely chopped fresh or frozen rhubarb, thawed and drained

TOPPING
- 6   oz. cream cheese, softened
- ½   cup sugar
- ½   tsp. vanilla extract
- 1   cup heavy whipping cream, whipped

1. In a bowl, combine the flour and sugar; cut in butter until the mixture resembles coarse crumbs. Press into a greased 13x9-in. baking pan. Bake at 350° for 10 minutes.
2. Meanwhile, for filling, combine sugar and flour in a bowl. Whisk in cream and eggs. Stir in the rhubarb. Pour over crust. Bake at 350° until custard is set, 40-45 minutes. Cool.
3. For topping, beat cream cheese, sugar and vanilla until smooth; fold in whipped cream. Spread over top. Cover and chill. Cut into bars. Store in the refrigerator.
1 BAR: 198 cal., 11g fat (7g sat. fat), 52mg chol., 70mg sod., 23g carb. (16g sugars, 1g fiber), 2g pro.

SMALL BATCH BROWNIES

Here's the perfect chocolaty treat for a small household. For a pretty accent, dust the tops with confectioners' sugar.
—*Taste of Home* Test Kitchen

PREP: 15 min. • **BAKE:** 15 min. + cooling
MAKES: 6 servings

- 2   Tbsp. butter
- ½   oz. unsweetened chocolate, chopped
- 1   large egg
- ¼   tsp. vanilla extract
- ⅔   cup sugar
- ⅓   cup all-purpose flour
- ¼   cup baking cocoa
- ¼   tsp. salt
- ¼   tsp. confectioners' sugar, optional

1. In a microwave, melt the butter and chocolate; stir until smooth. Cool slightly.
2. In a small bowl, whisk egg and vanilla; gradually whisk in sugar. Stir in chocolate mixture. Combine the flour, cocoa and salt; gradually add to chocolate mixture.
3. Transfer to a 9x5-in. loaf pan coated with cooking spray. Bake at 350° until a toothpick inserted in the center comes out clean, 12-16 minutes. Cool on a wire rack. Cut into bars. Dust with confectioners' sugar if desired.
1 BROWNIE: 179 cal., 6g fat (3g sat. fat), 45mg chol., 138mg sod., 30g carb. (23g sugars, 1g fiber), 3g pro. **DIABETIC EXCHANGES:** 2 starch, 1 fat.

RHUBARB CUSTARD BARS

**EASY FRESH
STRAWBERRY PIE
PAGE 102**

Desserts

The Test Kitchen is a sweet spot for the entire *Taste of Home* staff. The home economists have made many treasured recipes again and again, and they've shared the best here. From pies and cakes to tortes and trifles, these tried-and-true heavenly desserts make any meal ending extra special.

TIRAMISU TOFFEE TORTE

Tiramisu is Italian for *pick-me-up*, and this treat lives up to its name. The torte is truly worth every bit of effort. If you like, bake the cake in advance and split the layers, then freeze until you're ready to assemble it all.
—Donna Gonda, North Canton, OH

- -

PREP: 25 min. • **BAKE:** 25 min. + chilling
MAKES: 14 servings

- 1 pkg. white cake mix (regular size)
- 1 cup strong brewed coffee, room temperature
- 4 large egg whites
- 4 Heath candy bars (1.4 oz. each), chopped

FROSTING

- 4 oz. cream cheese, softened
- ⅔ cup sugar
- ⅓ cup chocolate syrup
- 2 tsp. vanilla extract
- 2 cups heavy whipping cream
- 6 Tbsp. strong brewed coffee, room temperature
- 1 Heath candy bar (1.4 oz.), chopped

1. Line two greased 9-in. round baking pans with waxed paper and grease the paper; set aside. In a large bowl, combine the cake mix, coffee and egg whites; beat on low speed for 30 seconds. Beat on medium for 2 minutes. Fold in chopped candy bars.

2. Pour into prepared pans. Bake at 350° for 25-30 minutes or until a toothpick inserted in the center comes out clean. Cool 10 minutes before removing to wire racks to cool.

3. For frosting, in a large bowl, beat the cream cheese and sugar until smooth. Beat in chocolate syrup and vanilla. Add the whipping cream. Beat on high speed until light and fluffy, about 5 minutes.

4. Cut each cake horizontally into two layers. Place the bottom layer on a serving plate; drizzle with 2 Tbsp. coffee. Spread with ¾ cup frosting. Repeat layers twice. Top with remaining cake layer. Frost top and sides of cake with remaining frosting. Refrigerate overnight. Garnish with chopped candy bar.

1 PIECE: 395 cal., 21g fat (12g sat. fat), 57mg chol., 305mg sod., 48g carb. (33g sugars, 1g fiber), 4g pro.

BLUEBERRY CHEESECAKE ICE CREAM

BLUEBERRY CHEESECAKE ICE CREAM

After sampling this flavor at an ice cream stand, I kept trying to duplicate it until it was just right.
—Melissa Symington, Neche, ND

- -

PREP: 55 min. + chilling
PROCESS: 20 min. + freezing
MAKES: 2 qt.

- ½ cup sugar
- 1 Tbsp. cornstarch
- ½ cup water
- 1¼ cups fresh or frozen blueberries
- 1 Tbsp. lemon juice

GRAHAM CRACKER MIXTURE

- 2¼ cups graham cracker crumbs (about 36 squares)
- 2 Tbsp. sugar
- ½ tsp. ground cinnamon
- ½ cup butter, melted

ICE CREAM

- 1½ cups sugar
- 1 pkg. (3.4 oz.) instant cheesecake or vanilla pudding mix
- 1 qt. heavy whipping cream
- 2 cups milk
- 2 tsp. vanilla extract

1. In a small saucepan, combine sugar and cornstarch. Gradually stir in water until smooth. Stir in blueberries and lemon juice. Bring to a boil over medium-high heat. Reduce heat; simmer, uncovered, for 5 minutes or until slightly thickened, stirring occasionally. Cover and refrigerate until chilled.

2. In a large bowl, combine the cracker crumbs, sugar and cinnamon. Stir in butter. Pat into an ungreased 15x10-in. baking pan. Bake at 350° until lightly browned, 10-15 minutes. Cool completely on a wire rack.

3. Meanwhile, in a large bowl, whisk the ice cream ingredients. Fill ice cream freezer cylinder two-thirds full; freeze according to manufacturer's directions. Refrigerate remaining mixture until ready to freeze. Whisk before adding to ice cream freezer (mixture will have some lumps).

4. Crumble the graham cracker mixture. In a large container, layer the ice cream, graham cracker mixture and blueberry sauce three times; swirl. Freeze.

½ CUP: 459 cal., 30g fat (18g sat. fat), 101mg chol., 252mg sod., 47g carb. (37g sugars, 1g fiber), 3g pro.

OLD-FASHIONED CUSTARD PIE

This lovely standby is always a comforting favorite at my house. Prepare dough for a double-crust pie if you want to make a braided crust edge; otherwise, simply prepare a single-crust pie dough and flute it as you traditionally would.
—Maxine Linkenauger, Montverde, FL

PREP: 20 min. + chilling
BAKE: 25 min. + chilling
MAKES: 8 servings

Pastry for single-crust pie (9 in.)
4 large eggs
2½ cups whole milk
½ cup sugar
1 tsp. ground nutmeg
1 tsp. vanilla extract
1 tsp. almond extract
½ tsp. salt

1. Unroll crust into a 9-in. pie plate; flute the edge. Refrigerate 30 minutes. Preheat oven to 400°.

2. Line unpricked crust with a double thickness of foil. Fill with pie weights, dried beans or uncooked rice. Bake on a lower oven rack 10-15 minutes or until edges are golden brown. Remove foil and weights; bake 3-6 minutes longer or until bottom is golden brown. Cool on a wire rack.

3. In a large bowl, whisk eggs. Whisk in remaining ingredients until blended. Pour into crust. Cover edges with foil. Bake at 400° for 25-30 minutes or until a knife inserted in the center comes out clean.

4. Cool on a wire rack for 1 hour. Refrigerate pie for at least 3 hours before cutting and serving. Refrigerate leftovers.

1 SLICE: 258 cal., 12g fat (5g sat. fat), 122mg chol., 317mg sod., 30g carb. (17g sugars, 0 fiber), 7g pro.

CHOCOLATE PEANUT PIE

Who can resist a tempting chocolate crumb crust and a creamy filling with big peanut butter flavor? Be prepared to take an empty plate home when you serve this pie at your next potluck.
—Doris Doherty, Albany, OR

PREP: 20 min. + cooling
MAKES: 10 servings

1¼ cups chocolate cookie
     crumbs (20 cookies)
¼ cup sugar
¼ cup butter, melted
FILLING
1 pkg. (8 oz.) cream cheese, softened
1 cup creamy peanut butter
1 cup sugar
1 Tbsp. butter, softened
1 tsp. vanilla extract
1 cup heavy whipping cream, whipped
     Grated chocolate or chocolate
     cookie crumbs, optional

1. In a small bowl, combine the cookie crumbs and sugar; stir in butter. Press onto the bottom and up the sides of a 9-in. pie plate. Bake at 375° for 10 minutes. Cool on a wire rack.

2. For filling, beat the cream cheese, peanut butter, sugar, butter and vanilla in a large bowl until smooth. Fold in whipped cream. Gently spoon into the crust. Garnish with chocolate or cookie crumbs if desired. Store in refrigerator.

1 SLICE: 551 cal., 39g fat (18g sat. fat), 73mg chol., 349mg sod., 44g carb. (34g sugars, 3g fiber), 10g pro.

OLD-FASHIONED
CUSTARD PIE

MOCHA TRUFFLE CHEESECAKE

EASY FRESH STRAWBERRY PIE

For my mother's 70th birthday, I made two of these strawberry pies instead of a cake. Since it was mid-May in Texas, the berries were absolutely perfect. It was a memorable occasion for the whole family.
—Josh Carter, Birmingham, AL

- -

PREP: 20 min. + cooling
BAKE: 15 min. + chilling
MAKES: 8 servings

  1 pastry shell, unbaked (9 in.)
  ¾ cup sugar
  2 Tbsp. cornstarch
  1 cup water
  1 pkg. (3 oz.) strawberry gelatin
  4 cups sliced fresh strawberries
     Whipped cream, optional

1. Line unpricked crust with a double thickness of heavy-duty foil. Bake at 450° for 8 minutes. Remove foil; bake 5 minutes longer. Cool on a wire rack.
2. In a small saucepan, combine the sugar, cornstarch and water until smooth. Bring to a boil; cook and stir for 2 minutes or until thickened. Remove from the heat; stir in gelatin until dissolved. Refrigerate for 15-20 minutes or until slightly cooled.
3. Meanwhile, arrange strawberries in the crust. Pour gelatin mixture over berries. Refrigerate until set. Serve with whipped cream if desired.
1 SLICE: 264 cal., 7g fat (3g sat. fat), 5mg chol., 125mg sod., 49g carb. (32g sugars, 2g fiber), 2g pro.

TEST KITCHEN TIP
For a different presentation, use whole fresh strawberries and arrange them pointed side up in the pastry shell. This is also a smart time-saver because you don't have to slice the berries.

MOCHA TRUFFLE CHEESECAKE

I went through a phase when I couldn't get enough cheesecake or coffee, so I created this rich dessert. Its brownie-like crust and creamy mocha layer really hit the spot. It's ideal for get-togethers because it can be made in advance.
—Shannon Dormady, Great Falls, MT

- -

PREP: 20 min. • **BAKE:** 50 min. + chilling
MAKES: 16 servings

  1 pkg. devil's food cake
     mix (regular size)
  6 Tbsp. butter, melted
  1 large egg
  1 to 3 Tbsp. instant coffee granules
FILLING/TOPPING
  2 pkg. (8 oz. each) cream cheese,
     softened
  1 can (14 oz.) sweetened
     condensed milk
  2 cups (12 oz.) semisweet chocolate
     chips, melted and cooled
  3 to 6 Tbsp. instant coffee granules
  ¼ cup hot water
  3 large eggs, lightly beaten
  1 cup heavy whipping cream
  ¼ cup confectioners' sugar
  ½ tsp. almond extract
  1 Tbsp. baking cocoa, optional

1. In a large bowl, combine the cake mix, butter, egg and coffee granules until well blended. Press onto the bottom and 2 in. up the sides of a greased 10-in. springform pan.
2. In another large bowl, beat cream cheese until smooth. Beat in milk and melted chips. Dissolve coffee granules in water; add to cream cheese mixture. Add eggs; beat on low speed just until combined. Pour into crust. Place pan on a baking sheet.
3. Bake at 325° for 50-55 minutes or until center is almost set. Cool on a wire rack for 10 minutes. Carefully run a knife around edge of pan to loosen; cool 1 hour longer. Chill overnight.
4. Just before serving, in a large bowl, beat cream until soft peaks form. Beat in sugar and extract until stiff peaks form. Spread over top of cheesecake. Sprinkle with cocoa if desired. Refrigerate leftovers.
1 SLICE: 484 cal., 28g fat (16g sat. fat), 109mg chol., 389mg sod., 55g carb. (41g sugars, 2g fiber), 7g pro.

EASY FRESH
STRAWBERRY PIE

POTLUCK GERMAN APPLE CAKE

My mother made this cake for my brothers and me when we were kids. It's an excellent choice for potlucks any time of year.
—Edie DeSpain, Logan, UT

- -

PREP: 15 min. • **BAKE:** 55 min. + cooling
MAKES: 16 servings

- 3 large eggs
- 2 cups sugar
- 1 cup vegetable oil
- 1 tsp. vanilla extract
- 2 cups all-purpose flour
- 2 tsp. ground cinnamon
- 1 tsp. baking soda
- ½ tsp. salt
- 4 cups chopped peeled tart apples
- ¾ cup chopped pecans

FROSTING
- 1 pkg. (8 oz.) cream cheese, softened
- 2 tsp. butter, softened
- 2 cups confectioners' sugar

1. In a large bowl, beat the eggs, sugar, oil and vanilla. Combine the flour, cinnamon, baking soda and salt; add to egg mixture and mix well. Fold in apples and nuts. Pour into a greased 13x9-in. baking dish. Bake at 350° for 55-60 minutes or until a toothpick inserted in the center comes out clean. Cool on a wire rack.

2. In a small bowl, beat cream cheese and butter. Add confectioners' sugar, beating until smooth. Spread over cake. Refrigerate the leftovers.

1 PIECE: 455 cal., 24g fat (6g sat. fat), 57mg chol., 212mg sod., 57g carb. (42g sugars, 2g fiber), 4g pro.

MAMAW EMILY'S
STRAWBERRY CAKE

MAMAW EMILY'S STRAWBERRY CAKE

My husband loved his Mamaw's strawberry cake. He thought no one could duplicate it. I made it, and it's just as scrumptious as he remembers.
—Jennifer Bruce, Manitou, KY

- -

PREP: 15 min. • **BAKE:** 25 min. + cooling
MAKES: 12 servings

- 1 pkg. white cake mix (regular size)
- 1 pkg. (3 oz.) strawberry gelatin
- 3 Tbsp. sugar
- 3 Tbsp. all-purpose flour
- 1 cup water
- ½ cup canola oil
- 2 large eggs
- 1 cup finely chopped strawberries

FROSTING
- ½ cup butter, softened
- ½ cup crushed strawberries
- 4½ to 5 cups confectioners' sugar

1. Preheat oven to 350°. Line the bottoms of two greased 8-in. round baking pans with parchment; grease paper.

2. In a large bowl, combine cake mix, gelatin, sugar and flour. Add water, oil and eggs; beat on low speed 30 seconds. Beat on medium 2 minutes. Fold in chopped strawberries. Transfer to prepared pans.

3. Bake 25-30 minutes or until a toothpick inserted in center comes out clean. Cool in pans for roughly 10 minutes before removing to wire racks; remove paper. Cool completely.

4. For frosting, in a small bowl, beat butter until creamy. Beat in crushed strawberries. Gradually beat in enough confectioners' sugar to reach desired consistency. Spread frosting between layers and over top and sides of cake.

1 SLICE: 532 cal., 21g fat (7g sat. fat), 51mg chol., 340mg sod., 85g carb. (69g sugars, 1g fiber), 4g pro.

TEST KITCHEN TIP
You'll be smitten with the nostalgic charm of this rich pink buttercream frosting, but for a change of pace, try icing the cake with whipped cream or whipped topping and serve with fresh berries. Save the prettiest strawberries for garnishing. Use second-tier berries for the cake interior and frosting.

SHOOFLY PIE

My grandmother made shoofly pie in the tradition of the Pennsylvania Dutch. If you haven't tried it, this recipe is a great start.
—Mark Morgan, Waterford, WI

- -

PREP: 20 min. + chilling
BAKE: 65 min. + cooling • **MAKES:** 8 servings

    Pastry for single-crust pie (9 in.)
½   cup packed brown sugar
½   cup molasses
1   large egg
1½ tsp. all-purpose flour
½   tsp. baking soda
1   cup boiling water
1   large egg yolk, lightly beaten
TOPPING
1½ cups all-purpose flour
¾   cup packed brown sugar
¾   tsp. baking soda
    Dash salt
6   Tbsp. cold butter, cubed

1. On a floured surface, roll dough to fit a 9-in. deep-dish pie plate. Trim and flute edge. Refrigerate at least 30 minutes.
2. Meanwhile, preheat oven to 425°. For the filling, mix brown sugar, molasses, egg, flour and baking soda. Gradually stir in boiling water; cool completely.
3. Line unpricked crust with a double thickness of foil. Fill with pie weights, dried beans or uncooked rice. Bake on a lower oven rack 15 minutes. Remove the foil and pie weights; brush crust with egg yolk. Bake 5 minutes. Cool on a wire rack. Reduce oven setting to 350°.
4. In another bowl, whisk together the first four topping ingredients. Cut in butter until crumbly. Add filling to crust; sprinkle with topping. Cover edge of pie with foil.
5. Bake until filling is set and golden brown, 45-50 minutes. Cool on a wire rack. Store in the refrigerator.
NOTE: Let pie weights cool before storing. Beans and rice may be reused for pie weights, but not for cooking.
1 SLICE: 540 cal., 22g fat (13g sat. fat), 99mg chol., 630mg sod., 82g carb. (49g sugars, 1g fiber), 6g pro.
PASTRY FOR SINGLE-CRUST PIE (9 IN.): Combine 1¼ cups all-purpose flour and ¼ tsp. salt; cut in ½ cup cold butter until crumbly. Gradually add 3-5 Tbsp. ice water, tossing with a fork until dough holds together when pressed. Wrap in plastic and refrigerate 1 hour.

CREME BRULEE

My favorite dessert is creme brulee, so I quickly learned how to successfully make this. Recently I was at a party where guests finished prepping their own desserts by broiling the sugar on the portions with small torches. What a clever idea!
—Joylyn Trickel, Helendale, CA

- -

PREP: 30 min. • **BAKE:** 45 min. + cooling
MAKES: 8 servings

4   cups heavy whipping cream
9   large egg yolks
¾   cup sugar
1   tsp. vanilla extract
    Brown sugar

1. In a large saucepan, combine the cream, egg yolks and sugar. Cook and stir over medium heat until mixture reaches 160° or is thick enough to coat the back of a metal spoon. Stir in vanilla.
2. Transfer to eight 6-oz. ramekins or custard cups. Place cups in a baking pan; add 1 in. of boiling water to pan. Bake, uncovered, at 325° for 25-30 minutes or until centers are just set (mixture will jiggle). Remove ramekins from water bath; cool for 10 minutes. Cover and refrigerate for at least 4 hours.
3. One hour before serving, place custards on a baking sheet. Sprinkle each with 1-2 tsp. brown sugar. Broil 8 in. from the heat for 4-7 minutes or until sugar is caramelized. Refrigerate leftovers.
1 SERVING: 551 cal., 50g fat (29g sat. fat), 402mg chol., 53mg sod., 22g carb. (22g sugars, 0 fiber), 6g pro.

SHOOFLY PIE

FROZEN MOCHA TORTE

For an easy, make-ahead dessert that's elegant and luscious, try this recipe. Each cool, refreshing slice has the perfect blend of mocha and chocolate.
—Aelita Kivirist, Glenview, IL

PREP: 20 min. + freezing
MAKES: 12 servings

- 1 cup chocolate wafer crumbs
- ¼ cup sugar
- ¼ cup butter, melted
- 1 pkg. (8 oz.) cream cheese, softened
- 1 can (14 oz.) sweetened condensed milk
- ⅔ cup chocolate syrup
- 2 Tbsp. instant coffee granules
- 1 Tbsp. hot water
- 1 cup heavy whipping cream, whipped

Chocolate-covered coffee beans, optional

1. In a small bowl, combine the wafer crumbs, sugar and butter. Press onto the bottom and 1 in. up the sides of a greased 9-in. springform pan; set aside.
2. In a large bowl, beat the cream cheese, milk and chocolate syrup until smooth. Dissolve coffee granules in hot water; add to cream cheese mixture. Fold in whipped cream. Pour over crust. Cover and freeze for 8 hours or overnight.
3. Remove from the freezer 10-15 minutes before serving. Carefully run a knife around edge of pan to loosen. Remove sides of pan. Garnish with coffee beans if desired.
1 SLICE: 414 cal., 23g fat (14g sat. fat), 74mg chol., 222mg sod., 47g carb. (39g sugars, 1g fiber), 6g pro.

POT OF S'MORES

Mom's easy Dutch oven version of the popular campout treat is so good and gooey. The hardest part was waiting for it to cool so we could devour it. Yum!
—June Dress, Meridian, ID

TAKES: 25 min. • **MAKES:** 12 servings

- 1 pkg. (14½ oz.) whole graham crackers, crushed
- ½ cup butter, melted
- 1 can (14 oz.) sweetened condensed milk
- 2 cups (12 oz.) semisweet chocolate chips
- 1 cup butterscotch chips
- 2 cups miniature marshmallows

1. Prepare grill or campfire for low heat, using 16-18 charcoal briquettes or large wood chips.
2. Line a Dutch oven with heavy-duty aluminum foil. Combine cracker crumbs and butter; press onto the bottom of the pan. Pour milk over crust and sprinkle with chocolate and butterscotch chips. Top with marshmallows.
3. Cover Dutch oven. When briquettes or wood chips are covered with white ash, place Dutch oven directly on top of six of them. Using long-handled tongs, place remaining briquettes on pan cover.
4. Cook for 15 minutes or until the miniature marshmallows begin to melt. To check for doneness, use the tongs to carefully lift the cover.
1 SERVING: 584 cal., 28g fat (17g sat. fat), 31mg chol., 326mg sod., 83g carb. (47g sugars, 3g fiber), 8g pro.

FROZEN MOCHA TORTE

BUTTERMILK LEMON
MERINGUE PIE

PUMPKIN-BUTTERSCOTCH
GINGERBREAD TRIFLE

There's more to pumpkin than pie, as this impressive trifle points out. It looks so fancy with alternating layers of cake and pumpkin/butterscotch pudding. Try making it ahead of time for a fuss-free dessert when you're planning to entertain guests.
—Lyla Lehenbauer, New London, MO

- -

PREP: 40 min. • **BAKE:** 35 min. + cooling
MAKES: 16 servings

1 pkg. (14½ oz.) gingerbread
   cake/cookie mix
4 cups cold fat-free milk
4 pkg. (1 oz. each) sugar-free instant
   butterscotch pudding mix
1 tsp. ground cinnamon
¼ tsp. ground ginger
¼ tsp. ground nutmeg
¼ tsp. ground allspice
1 can (15 oz.) pumpkin
1 carton (12 oz.) frozen reduced-
   fat whipped topping, thawed

1. Prepare and bake gingerbread mix according to package directions for cake. Cool completely.
2. Break cake into crumbles; reserve ¼ cup crumbs. In a large bowl, whisk milk, pudding mixes and spices until mixture is thickened, about 2 minutes. Stir in pumpkin.
3. In a 3½-qt. trifle or glass bowl, layer one-fourth of the cake crumbs, half of the pumpkin mixture, one-fourth of the cake crumbs and half of the whipped topping; repeat layers. Top with reserved crumbs. Refrigerate until serving.
¾ CUP: 220 cal., 6g fat (3g sat. fat), 13mg chol., 325mg sod., 33g carb. (18g sugars, 1g fiber), 4g pro. **DIABETIC EXCHANGES:** 2 starch, 1 fat.

BUTTERMILK
LEMON MERINGUE PIE

For lemon lovers everywhere, this pie, with a little tang, beats lemon meringue every time. There's just no contest. Compliments roll in whenever I serve it.
—Ellen Riley, Murfreesboro, TN

- -

PREP: 30 min. • **BAKE:** 15 min. + chilling
MAKES: 8 servings

1½ cups graham cracker crumbs
¼ cup sugar
⅓ cup butter, melted
FILLING
¾ cup sugar
3 Tbsp. cornstarch
1½ cups buttermilk
3 large egg yolks
2 Tbsp. butter
2 Tbsp. lemon juice
2 tsp. grated lemon zest
MERINGUE
3 large egg whites
½ tsp. vanilla extract
¼ tsp. cream of tartar
6 Tbsp. sugar

1. Combine the cracker crumbs, sugar and butter; press onto the bottom and up the sides of an ungreased 9-in. pie plate. Bake at 350° for 10-12 minutes or until crust is lightly browned. Cool on a wire rack.
2. For filling, in a large saucepan, combine sugar and cornstarch. Stir in buttermilk until smooth. Cook and stir over medium-high heat until thickened and bubbly. Reduce heat to low; cook and stir for 2 minutes longer. Remove from the heat. Stir 1 cup of hot mixture into egg yolks; return all to pan, stirring constantly. Bring to a gentle boil; cook and stir for 2 minutes longer. Remove from the heat. Stir in butter. Gently stir in lemon juice and zest. Pour hot filling into the crust.
3. For meringue, in a small mixing bowl, beat the egg whites, vanilla and cream of tartar on medium speed until soft peaks form. Gradually beat in sugar, 1 Tbsp. at a time, on high until stiff peaks form. Spread over hot filling, sealing edges to crust.
4. Bake for 15-20 minutes or until golden brown. Cool on a wire rack for 1 hour; refrigerate for 1-2 hours before serving. Refrigerate leftovers.
1 SLICE: 350 cal., 14g fat (8g sat. fat), 106mg chol., 242mg sod., 52g carb. (42g sugars, 1g fiber), 5g pro.

CHOCOLATE
CREAM PIE

CHOCOLATE CREAM PIE

Our son, John, did a lot of 4-H baking as a teenager. His favorite is this old-fashioned creamy chocolate pudding in a flaky crust.
—Mary Anderson, De Valls Bluff, AR

PREP: 1¼ hours + chilling
MAKES: 8 servings

- 1½ cups sugar
- ⅓ cup all-purpose flour
- 3 Tbsp. baking cocoa
- ½ tsp. salt
- 1½ cups water
- 1 can (12 oz.) evaporated milk
- 5 large egg yolks, lightly beaten
- ½ cup butter
- 1 tsp. vanilla extract
- 1 pastry shell (9 in.), baked
  Whipped topping and baking cocoa, optional

1. In a large saucepan, combine the first six ingredients. Cook and stir over medium-high heat for 2 minutes or until thickened and bubbly. Reduce heat; cook and stir 2 minutes longer. Remove from the heat. Whisk 1 cup hot mixture into egg yolks. Return all to the pan; bring to a gentle boil, stirring constantly.
2. Remove from the heat; stir in butter and vanilla. Cool slightly. Pour warm filling into the crust. Cool for 1 hour. Chill until set. If desired, top with whipped cream and sprinkle with cocoa to serve.
1 SLICE: 488 cal., 25g fat (13g sat. fat), 184mg chol., 413mg sod., 60g carb. (42g sugars, 1g fiber), 7g pro.

READER RAVE
"This is the best chocolate pie I've ever had! Family could tell right away it was homemade and not instant pudding mix. I just used a graham cracker crust for it, and it could really make two pies! Sometimes, I use the extra filling to make little cup desserts, layering the pudding and the whipped cream. Yummy!"
—LUIGIMON, TASTEOFHOME.COM

STRAWBERRY/RHUBARB CRUMB PIE

STRAWBERRY/RHUBARB CRUMB PIE

Everyone seems to have a rhubarb patch in Maine, and this is a delicious way to enjoy it. The pie won first prize at our church fair; I hope it's a winner at your house, too!
—Paula Phillips, East Winthrop, ME

PREP: 15 min. • **BAKE:** 45 min.
MAKES: 8 servings

- 1 large egg
- 1 cup sugar
- 2 Tbsp. all-purpose flour
- 1 tsp. vanilla extract
- ¾ lb. rhubarb ribs, cut into ½-in. pieces, or sliced frozen rhubarb (about 3 cups)
- 1 pint fresh strawberries, halved
- 1 unbaked pie shell (9 in.)

TOPPING
- ¾ cup all-purpose flour
- ½ cup packed brown sugar
- ½ cup quick-cooking or old-fashioned oats
- ½ cup cold butter, cubed

1. In a large bowl, beat egg. Beat in the sugar, flour and vanilla until well blended. Gently stir in rhubarb and strawberries. Pour into the crust.
2. For topping, in a small bowl, combine the flour, brown sugar and oats; cut in butter until crumbly. Sprinkle over fruit.
3. Bake at 400° for 10 minutes. Reduce heat to 350°; bake for 35 minutes longer or until crust is golden brown and filling is bubbly. Cool on a wire rack.
NOTE: If using frozen rhubarb, measure rhubarb while still frozen, then thaw completely. Drain in a colander, but do not press liquid out.
1 SLICE: 468 cal., 20g fat (10g sat. fat), 62mg chol., 232mg sod., 70g carb. (42g sugars, 2g fiber), 5g pro.

LOVELY LEMON CHEESECAKE

Wait for the oohs and aahs when you present this luxurious cheesecake. The lemon flavor gives it a bright and tangy flair.
—Margaret Allen, Abingdon, VA

PREP: 25 min. • **BAKE:** 70 min. + chilling
MAKES: 14 servings

- ¾ cup graham cracker crumbs
- 2 Tbsp. sugar
- 3 tsp. ground cinnamon
- 2 Tbsp. butter, melted

FILLING

- 5 pkg. (8 oz. each) cream cheese, softened
- 1⅔ cups sugar
- ⅛ tsp. salt
- ¼ cup lemon juice
- 1½ tsp. vanilla extract
- 5 large eggs, lightly beaten
  Thin lemon slices, optional

1. Preheat oven to 325°. Place a greased 10-in. springform pan on a double thickness of heavy-duty foil (about 18 in. square). Wrap foil securely around pan.

2. In a small bowl, mix cracker crumbs, sugar and cinnamon; stir in butter. Press onto bottom of prepared pan; refrigerate while preparing filling.

3. In a large bowl, beat cream cheese, sugar and salt until smooth. Beat in lemon juice and vanilla. Add eggs; beat on low speed just until blended. Pour over crust. Place the springform pan in a larger baking pan; add 1 in. of hot water to larger pan.

4. Bake 70-80 minutes or until center is just set and top appears dull. Remove springform pan from water bath. Cool cheesecake on a wire rack 10 minutes. Loosen sides from pan with a knife; remove foil. Cool 1 hour longer. Refrigerate overnight, covering the pan when completely cooled.

5. Remove rim from pan. If desired, top cheesecake with lemon slices.

1 SLICE: 444 cal., 32g fat (19g sat. fat), 169mg chol., 325mg sod., 32g carb. (27g sugars, 0 fiber), 9g pro.

CHOCOLATE CHEESECAKE PIE

CHOCOLATE CHEESECAKE PIE

Guests always go for this rich but simple pie. I like topping it with fresh raspberries or a little cherry pie filling.
—Sandy Schwartz, Brooklyn, NY

TAKES: 30 min. • **MAKES:** 8 servings

- 1 pkg. (8 oz.) cream cheese, softened
- ¼ cup butter, softened
- ⅓ cup sugar
- 1½ tsp. vanilla extract
- 1½ cups milk chocolate chips, melted and cooled
- 1 carton (8 oz.) frozen whipped topping, thawed
- 1 graham cracker crust (9 in.)
  Chocolate curls, optional

In a large bowl, beat cream cheese, butter, sugar and vanilla until smooth. Beat in the cooled chocolate. Fold in the whipped topping. Spoon into crust. Refrigerate until serving. Decorate with chocolate curls as desired.

1 SLICE: 535 cal., 35g fat (20g sat. fat), 53mg chol., 270mg sod., 48g carb. (38g sugars, 1g fiber), 6g pro.

CHOCOLATE SAUCE

I make my own ice cream toppings so my family can enjoy our favorite snack: banana splits. This smooth chocolate fudge sauce is always a big hit.
—Nancy McDonald, Burns, WY

TAKES: 15 min. • **MAKES:** About 3⅓ cups

- ½ cup butter
- 2 oz. unsweetened chocolate
- 2 cups sugar
- 1 cup half-and-half cream or evaporated milk
- ½ cup light corn syrup
- 1 tsp. vanilla extract

1. In a large heavy saucepan, melt butter and chocolate; stir until smooth. Add the sugar, cream and corn syrup. Bring to a boil, stirring constantly. Boil for 1½ minutes. Remove from the heat.

2. Stir in vanilla. Serve warm or cold over ice cream or pound cake. Refrigerate leftovers.

2 TBSP.: 127 cal., 5g fat (3g sat. fat), 14mg chol., 48mg sod., 21g carb. (18g sugars, 0 fiber), 0 pro.

BLACK WALNUT LAYER CAKE

My sister gave me this recipe years ago. The thin layer of frosting spread on the sides gives it a chic modern look.
—Lynn Glaze, Warren, OH

- -

PREP: 25 min. • **BAKE:** 20 min. + cooling
MAKES: 16 servings

- ½ cup butter, softened
- ½ cup shortening
- 2 cups sugar
- 2 tsp. vanilla extract
- 4 large eggs, room temperature
- 3¾ cups all-purpose flour
- 2 tsp. baking soda
- ½ tsp. salt
- 1½ cups buttermilk
- 1¼ cups finely chopped black or English walnuts

FROSTING
- ½ cup butter, softened
- 1 pkg. (8 oz.) cream cheese, softened
- 1 tsp. vanilla extract
- 4½ cups confectioners' sugar
- 1 to 3 Tbsp. buttermilk
  Additional black walnuts
  Thin orange slices, optional

1. Preheat oven to 350°. Line bottoms of three greased 9-in. round baking pans with parchment; grease paper.
2. Cream butter, shortening and sugar until light and fluffy. Add vanilla and eggs, one at a time, beating well after each addition. In another bowl, whisk together flour, baking soda and salt; add to creamed mixture alternately with buttermilk, beating after each addition. Fold in walnuts.
3. Transfer to prepared pans. Bake until a toothpick inserted in center comes out clean, 20-25 minutes. Cool in pans for 10 minutes before removing to wire racks; remove paper. Cool completely.
4. For frosting, beat butter and cream cheese until smooth. Beat in the vanilla. Gradually beat in confectioners' sugar and enough buttermilk to reach spreading consistency.
5. Spread 1 cup frosting between each cake layer. Spread top of cake with an additional 1 cup frosting. Spread remaining frosting in a thin layer over side of cake. Top with additional walnuts and, if desired, thin orange slices.
1 SLICE: 630 cal., 30g fat (13g sat. fat), 92mg chol., 432mg sod., 84g carb. (60g sugars, 1g fiber), 9g pro.

CHOCOLATE SOUFFLES

Try these easy-to-make souffles for your next dinner party. The mini servings have a maximum portion of deliciousness!
—Sarah Farmer, Culinary Director

- -

PREP: 20 min. • **BAKE:** 15 min.
MAKES: 6 servings

- 4 large eggs
- 6 tsp. plus 1 Tbsp. sugar, divided
- 1 cup light corn syrup
- ½ cup baking cocoa
- 1 tsp. vanilla extract
  Confectioners' sugar

1. Separate eggs; let stand at room temperature for 30 minutes. Coat six 6-oz. souffle dishes with cooking spray. Sprinkle 1 tsp. sugar into each dish, tilting to cover the bottom and sides; set aside.
2. Preheat oven to 375°. In a large bowl, whisk corn syrup, cocoa, egg yolks and vanilla until blended; set aside. In a large bowl with clean beaters, beat egg whites on medium speed until soft peaks form. Gradually beat in remaining sugar on high until stiff peaks form. Gently fold a fourth of the egg white mixture into the chocolate mixture; fold in remaining egg white mixture.
3. Spoon batter into prepared dishes. Bake 15-20 minutes or until a toothpick inserted in the center comes out clean. Dust with confectioners' sugar. Serve warm.
1 SOUFFLE: 250 cal., 4g fat (1g sat. fat), 142mg chol., 108mg sod., 53g carb. (34g sugars, 1g fiber), 5g pro.

BLACK WALNUT LAYER CAKE

RECIPE INDEX